Transformations
Children's meaning making in a nursery

Transformations
Children's meaning making in a nursery

Kate Pahl

Trentham Books

First published in 1999 by Trentham Books Limited

Trentham Books Limited
Westview House
734 London Road
Oakhill
Stoke on Trent
Staffordshire
England ST4 5NP

British Cataloguing in Publication Data
A catalogue record for this book is available from the British Library

ISBN 1 85856 098 5
(hb ISBN 1 85856 112 4)

Cover design by Aquarium Graphic Design

Designed and typeset by Trentham Print Design Ltd., Chester and printed in Great Britain by Cromwell Press Ltd, Wiltshire.

Contents

Acknowledgements • vii

Chapter 1
Introduction • 1

Chapter 2
Observation in action • 9

Chapter 3
Tracking the flow • 17
Seeds, baskets and shopping

Chapter 4
The third dimension • 35
Making things more real

Chapter 5
Seeing is believing • 55
Writing their names

Chapter 6
Try to see it my way • 73
Making a princess

Chapter 7
The Power Ranger is fighting the baddies • 87
Boys and meaning making

Chapter 8
Home and school • 101
Ideas for teachers and parents

Select bibliography • 107

Acknowledgements

This book would not have been possible without the help and support of the following people and institutions. I would like to thank:

Grasmere Primary School, in particular, Penny Greenhalgh, the Headteacher, who has been consistently positive, and Chris Luke, Nursery teacher and Lesley Ash, Nursery nurse who allowed me in and let me watch. I am also grateful for Chris and Lesley for taking some of the photographs in the book.

Gunther Kress, Institute of Education who has given a huge amount of supervision, support and inspiration. Judy Demaine, Institute of Education has supported my work through her kindness.

Myra Barrs, Centre for Language in Primary Education (CLPE) who supervised rigorously and supportively in the early stages of the work.

The National Literacy Trust, in particular my job share partner, Viv Bird.

The following people read the manuscript, contributed to the book or made helpful suggestions at crucial moments in the project: Julienne Ford, Helen Franks, Alison Joseph, Margaret Meek, Lou Opit, Jan Pahl, Ray Pahl, Idonea Taube, Cathy Troupp.

I would like to thank the children who worked with me and their parents who allowed me to use their work, especially:

Ziyaad and Zainab Achala, Georgia Ashton, Lucy Benjamin, Wilfie Boon, Mutahhara Choudhury, William Harvey, Martha Hilton, Andre Mason Malik, Abigail McNeill, Joseph Newman, Abdul Omar, Becky Potter, Jack Suckley, Lydia Sylvester.

I would also like to thank Dawn Mayne for her childcare support, and Molly for her arrival, Gillian Klein for her faith in the book and Martin for encouragement and support.

Dedicated to Isabel, Barney and Molly
who taught me to see

'Transformations *is an entirely enchanting and at the same time utterly precise account of the ways in which three year olds, in a nursery school, make sense of their world. Kate Pahl combines the joyful engagement of a parent with the clear eye of a researcher in a study which reveals the complexity of thinking and feeling in children's drawing, pasting, cutting out, and shows how this is totally bound up with their move into literacy. This book will make you see differently'.*
– Gunter Kress, Professor of Education/English,
Institute of Education, University of London

Chapter 1

Introduction

This book is for three groups of people. The first is anyone who has watched children between three and five years old drawing, writing or modelling, and has found that activity thought provoking. This could be the parent of a child who is starting to draw, or someone working in a nursery setting with children. It soon becomes obvious that children's models or drawings are highly significant to them. They mean a great deal, both in terms of what they are communicating, and in terms of what they tell us about the child's inner world. This book is written for that curious and interested group of people.

Secondly, it is addressed to literacy specialists who are concerned with developing literacy in young children. This book argues that literacy is a much deeper concept than the simple equation with the alphabet and reading and writing. Instead, the children in this study would move from modelling to beginning writing, and from drawing to telling stories, as if drawing and modelling were bound up with writing and telling stories. These activities are closely intertwined. Furthermore, literacy activities were seen to rest upon internal cultural assumptions which children brought to the activities they engaged upon. It is important to pay attention to children's assumptions about the self and about their world in order to understand fully and to develop children's literacy.

Thirdly, this book is intended also for policy makers. There is a move to extend formal full time education to four year old children. The intention behind this is partly to improve children's literacy development. However, this book suggests that four year olds need to work in a wide variety of mediums, including modelling, drawing and play activities as a 'way in' to developing literacy activities. Above all, it must be recognised where children are when they start to learn. In this I echo the work of many other researchers and practitioners in the early years settings.

I embarked upon this research as a parent of a three and a half year old boy in a school nursery so I could see how home and school interacted with each other. I combined my knowledge of close reading of texts with a background in research methods and methodology to set up a structure of close observation as the basis for my practice – which I describe in Chapter 2. This was accompanied by an exploration of children's texts as the basis for the study. Current literacy issues and practices illuminate the themes in the final two chapters, which look at boys and literacy and the linking of home and school. The book ends with an appeal to educators not to discount the informal and unstructured world of creating at home.

Plan of the book

The first two chapters introduce the reader to the principle of observation as a research method and provide background information about the research project. There follow four chapters based on observations on the process of representing the world through models, play and drawing. In Chapter 3, the fluidity and complexity of this process is explored. By looking at where ideas come from, and how they can be represented, we can begin to understand how children use drawing and models to explore concepts. The way in which ideas are expressed is crucial. Chapter 4 examines the significance of the move from two dimensional to three dimensional objects. This leads to a discussion of object making as an aid to play and to literacy development. I argue that children use space in a meaningful and motivated way but that the content of children's representations is dramatically different according to the cultural experience of each child. Chapter 5 discusses how children's model making is informed by cultural messages. I explore the influences behind much of children's drawing and model making, and emphasise the importance of recognising children's different social and cultural experiences. In Chapter 6 I look directly at literacy – at how children come to literacy and what they perceive literacy to be. All four chapters question the established focus on literacy as a skill linked to the alphabet and to the printed word. Instead, literacy is taken as part of a wider landscape of communication. The observations illuminate much contemporary nursery practice in that they support the work of nursery teachers who engage children in a wider variety of free modelling and drawing experiences.

In the last two chapters, I argue for a shift in practice, focusing particularly on:

- boys and literacy, and the need to recognise work which is constructed in space but which leads to narrative and literacy. Boys in particular tended to express ideas in terms of construction or modelling

- home and school and the importance of linking the two in facilitating model making and children's narratives. The importance for children of taking their work home, and of nursery teachers and parents working together to support children's narratives is emphasised.

Throughout the book, reference is made to current nursery practice. By lifting out and concentrating on a small part of what goes on in a nursery, I hope to support and illuminate the existing good practice going on in nursery classrooms.

Other studies of early literacy

Early literacy activities have been recorded and described very closely in a number of studies. Some studies develop the concept of literacy as linked to other activities such as writing and play. Many use observation of, for example, one child, to detail how children come to using literacy in their world, such as Glenda Bissex's book, *Gnys at Wrk: a Child Learns to Write and Read* (1980). Bissex observed one child's experience of early literacy and print, and through this observation examined the beginning of writing and phonetic spelling. Since the focus is on print, the wider experience of pre-literacy is not explored, but her book gives a fascinating account of a child's breakthrough into print, and also reveals the richness of the observation process. As parents or teachers and as people involved with children, we can use our experience of watching children to learn from them, and to develop theories about them. This is the strength of *Gnys at Wrk*. It teaches us to value observation and the collection of materials.

The pre-history of literacy and the links between drawing and writing have been examined by many researchers. Making marks as a symbolising activity has also been commented upon and described. In *Literacy before Schooling* (1982) Ferreiro and Teberosky explored how children's marks on a page develop, by systematically watching pre-school children. Again, this study gives value to watching what children do. The model the authors use has its origin in Piagetian thought, according to which children move through clearly defined 'stages'. Although my study does not employ this model, *Literacy before Schooling* offers valuable insight into pre-literacy and the symbols and signs children use to describe their world in the very earliest stage of their development.

While the observation of individual children's writing is a useful aid to understanding pre-literacy, the importance of the social environment to children's writing cannot be over-estimated. Anne Haas Dyson, in *The Social Worlds of Children Learning to Write* (1993) described how children's stories and narratives arose in the context of a wide range of activities, including play and drawing. Dyson's observations took place in an urban primary school, with a group of children from a number of different cultural backgrounds. She described how five year old children's texts were often a complex interweaving of oral narratives, drawing and writing, and that pulling apart these modes as separate entities often detracted from the power of the children's composing activities. She was able to see that writing on its own was different from writing with pictures, and to track how texts were produced and in what context. She is a strong believer in valuing what children bring to their writing and composing activities and in listening to the talk around composition. In that sense, Dyson offers a way of seeing texts as complex forms, often occurring in a number of modes, 'The written texts of five and six year olds are often multi-media affairs, interweavings of written words, spoken ones and pictures' (p.9). The book valued children's social worlds and taught us to listen to children's accounts of their experience. Dyson suggested that teachers need to honour their pupils' experience when developing writing activities. By looking at the totality of what children produced – the words, pictures and writing, with attention to the children's home life and play life – the child's productions were set in a context which made them relevant and comprehensible. I used the model she offers for valuing a wide spectrum of production when collecting material for this book.

Writing and drawing by young children is often accompanied by play. Many writers have stressed the importance of play as a developing and symbolising activity for children. Vivian Gussin Paley, in *Wally's Stories* (1980) and *Mollie is Three: growing up in school* (1986) described complex narrative play by young children. Influences from media, myth and fairytale were also acknowledged as important in Paley's analysis. She recognised that fantasy play has a crucial place in the development of thought in pre-schoolers. Carol Fox (in Hall and Martello 1996) also emphasises the importance of symbolising play in developing children's mental processes and linked this kind of play closely to storytelling and writing skills. Through her observations, she recognised the power of children's inner thoughts as expressed through play.

Play as observed in pre-school children is a complex weave of influences. Many observational studies have noted how easily children combine influences from television, videos, stories and toy characters. This switching between texts is a form of **intertextuality** – literally, between texts. Pre-school children combine texts readily, and are able to employ different modes to do so. Hilton (1996) argued for the valuing of children's popular culture, and the celebration of children's culture within the classroom.

Many teachers have observed that play has links with literacy. Children mimic adult behaviour in writing menus and pretending to write shopping lists. Children observe adults reading and writing and incorporate this into their play. Nigel Hall and Anne Robinson, in *Exploring Writing and Play in the Early Years* (1995) showed how play is a form of authoring which can be closely connected to writing activities. By charting such activities as running a restaurant or being a doctor or running a garage, the authors showed how children integrated their experience of literacy in their play. Literacy as an element of adult activity was seen as part of the children's play. The researchers showed how literacy activities rested on a large number of other activities, including play, and argued for a valuing of children's play within the classroom.

Early literacy activities rest on a complex sea of play, talk, writing, drawing and modelling, among other things. All are forms of representation. Many studies now recognise this, and seek to observe and listen to children in order to support the work they do when engaging with the world. *Listening to Children Think: exploring talk in the early years* (1996), edited by Nigel Hall and Julie Martello, developed this idea of listening to children's talk in order to support play and early literacy activities. Again, this process of engaging with the developing meanings of children yielded high returns in a classroom focused on developing children's literacy skills.

All these studies agree that literacy is meshed in with other activities, be they play, drawing, painting, modelling or speaking. In *Before Writing* (1997) Gunther Kress argues that children create their meanings in a multi-modal way. They employ the representational resources available to them at the time. Kress's book uses the language of semiotics to understand children's texts. He provides a dynamic view of how children make meaning, and, through a close examination of children's texts, offers an account of text making that takes into consideration the design of the object. Textual analysis of children's work is pushed further as Kress examines drawing and modelling in terms of form and content, and as a form of representation as powerful as composing and writing.

While offering different accounts of children's literacy, the studies share a common attention to what children produce and put this at the centre of the discussions. They also share an understanding of children's literacy that is dynamic and interactive. Literacy is not a static skill which children can acquire by simply learning the alphabet and sounding out words – it is a complex set of skills, meshed with other activities, which include emergent writing, the shape of letters, the beginning of telling stories, play and communication. All these authors use the word 'literacy' to describe a wide variety of activities, all connected but all focused on communication.

Understanding children's representation

Adults separate out different types of activity – drawing, writing, modelling, playing, construction activities and work. When I write a letter, I do not make a model of the thought I have within the letter before writing it. I am unlikely to draw the dish I make for supper or compose a bedtime story through play before telling it. I regard reading, cooking and writing as separate activities. However, when I observed the work of children in a nursery I saw the children take an idea and express it in different forms. For them, reading a book about a penguin was a small step to making a penguin suit. A project on shopping was manifested in shopping bags, baskets, lists and play. While this is a 'taken for granted' aspect of work in a nursery, it is also significant in revealing clues to how children's minds work. As active meaning makers they are able to employ different modes to express ideas. Just as adults make films or paint pictures to express their thoughts about the world, children use a variety of media to represent meaning. Many children come to the school nursery with developed expectations of their meaning making. So a home corner, water, sand and paint, are familiar from playgroup, while drawing and modelling are encountered within the early years curriculum. Many children want to spend their time at nursery drawing or modelling. However, as educators, nursery teachers are expected to engage the children in a variety of literacy-related activities, learning about how books can be read, writing and recognising their names. Schooling, even nursery schooling, is increasingly associated with literacy, in particular alphabetic script and books.

Yet when children make models or draw, they are developing the foundations of early literacy. They are dealing with the basic structures of representation. What they make is often influenced by stories they hear in the nursery, or experiences from home. The makers of models are also communicating. The children I observed often drew, painted and modelled in order to tell me about their worlds. Without having access to these ways they use to communicate, we would be unable to reach their developing thoughts and ideas. A rich pattern of meaning making already exists before children arrive at literacy.

What I describe here inevitably engages with the language of semiotics, which provides a useful tool to describe and analyse children's productions. Semiotics is the study of signs existing within a complex social and cultural space. Semiotics asserts that signs are products of the social environment in which they were produced. Later chapters demonstrate how this form of analysis reveals the rich complexity of children's sign making within the structures of their social and cultural environment. With this form of analysis it is possible to chart a pattern in children's drive to make signs through play and drawing and also in their inner experimentation with ideas and thoughts.

This leads us to examine children's work by asking questions about its form. Is the work in two-dimensional or three-dimensional form? What material is used? What is the shape? Have the materials been turned into systematic ways of representation, whether as images, gestures or models? These representational forms can be described as **modes**. Images are born within different modes of representation: on the page as drawing, collage, modelling or as gesture, play, speech or writing. When children make a sign, they do so within a particular mode of representation.

Reading Images: the grammar of visual design (Kress and van Leeuwen, 1996) emphasises the importance of a structural understanding of sign making in order to clarify the intentions of the maker and the audience. The book encourages us to consider aspects such as layout, directionality and structure as important aspects of a sign, whether the sign is a book, a leaflet or a sculpture. In a similar way, every production made by the children can be examined for its internal design structure. This book carefully examines the design of children's models to extend our understanding of the decisions children reach concerning form and structure.

When children make models they are driven by a complex web of impulses. One thing I wanted to know was, how children come to be interested and motivated to produce their signs. The importance of feelings or affect should not be underestimated. As I watched the children, I realised that their motivation to express a thought or create a person in a particular way, came from a complex combination of sources. Children grow up shaped by culture, but at the same time bring in their feelings about the world. Siblings, their parents, their feelings about their body and the world around them, come into play when children are communicating.

At the heart of many studies about the semiotics children use is an understanding that all children's writing, drawing, play and symbolising is shaped by the context in which they are produced and that this then shapes the form of the sign. So we understand a text such as a drawing within the context in which it was produced. As well as the precise circumstances of the making of the drawing or model, the talking that accompanied it, the play, stories and videos that preceded it, we also need to acknowledge the social and emotional factors at play while the model is being created. Some of these factors can be explained in terms of the child's home background or cultural life. But there is another whole area – the child's emotional life. Sometimes models can be explained with reference to a major event in their lives, such as the arrival of a new sibling. Powerful experiences, such as being very ill or losing a parent, may generate particular texts. All these factors bring meaning to a model. We cannot understand a child's line on a page without a great deal of information about them, the space they are in, their relationship to the page, and their intention while drawing that line. This process leads us into the world of psychology and an awareness that all acts exist within a social structure. Also helpful is the work of people who tried to understand the inner thoughts of children by using ideas from psychoanalysis. Children are driven by many deep impulses, some hidden, others more evident.

The stress in this book is on valuing what children bring to their making and composing activities in the classroom and how important it is that that activity is valued in the classroom. By examining children's texts minutely and offering an account of how they work, I hope to encourage teachers and parents to pay close attention to the activity going on around them. When we begin to unpack and examine what children do when they are making and drawing models, the complexity of their thoughts begins to unravel and a rich landscape of representation is revealed.

Chapter 2

Observation in action

Parents and people who work with three year old children in playgroups and nurseries are very privileged. They have access to the people who are working out what their world means to them. Pre-school children use a variety of media to communicate. We recognise this when we provide children with paint, talk to them, give them opportunities to play and dress up, encourage construction activities and make-believe – activities which may take place at home or in a playgroup, at a one o'clock club or a childminder's house. When we watch children in a playgroup or nursery we see how they move from one activity, such as painting, to another such as sticking, and then to building with bricks. These activities are all important in developing communication skills. For the child, they also represent meaning; the bricks are the medium through which the child is communicating. Construction or modelling can be valued as activities in themselves, just as important as drawing or writing. The challenge for us is to understand the difference between drawing with a pen on the page and working with glue and cardboard and to see where working in the third dimension changes an object. Uncovering the meanings behind a model ship or a basket gives us a window into children's pre-occupations and the narratives thay are currently focused on. It also allows us to understand how children engage with the form of the object, its construction.

In this chapter I argue for close observation as a way in to understanding how children express their ideas. I describe my study and offer some information about its context. This sets the scene for the next four chapters, which are concerned with the observations themselves. People working with young children should apply the information they can gather about their worlds through observing their drawings and models when they then develop work with young children.

When children receive an idea, they take it in and it becomes meaningful to them. For example, from one nursery child's interest in the story of *Peter Pan* came the idea to make a Captain Hook's hook out of the inside of a toilet roll. This idea spread and the children became pre-occupied with making hooks. In another observation, the children made wings to become the fairy Tinkerbell. It is possible to track the process of hearing the story of *Peter Pan* to the making of the models. Children may also be observed acting out the story of *Peter Pan* and adapting it to become part of further play and model making. Children take ideas on and transform them in their own unique ways. Through watching children listen to stories, make models, draw and write, we can uncover a fascinating and complex understanding of how ideas can be received and translated into completely different activities.

The way I discovered this was through closely observing everything a group of children were hearing, doing and making when I observed a nursery class in a small inner city school for one term. I visited the classroom for two hours a week and recorded everything that happened in that period. I took away some of the models and drawings that the children created, or took photographs of what they produced. While I watched the children, I took brief notes of what I was seeing. When I left the nursery, I wrote up the sessions I watched in detail; these are the Observation Notes referred to in the book. I then reflected on these notes and worked with them to understand what the children were doing. The notes, together with the texts I took away and the information I collected from parents and teachers, make up the data presented in this book. I had a place in the classroom because my child was in the nursery, and this affected the data, as the children saw me as a parent who came and worked with them from time to time. Finally, I re-visited the nursery for a longer time and developed further work with individual children. This extended work took place over about a year and the data collected is also presented here. Not all the texts discussed in this book were made by the children in the classroom – they made some of them at home.

Background to the research

The small inner city school had children from a number of different linguistic, religious and cultural backgrounds including Somalia, Bangladesh and Turkey. Some had come as refugees and there was a variety of religious backgrounds. The children started part time just after their third birthday and stayed in the nursery till they were four and a half but most of the children I studied were between three and a half and four years old.

The nursery had a carefully planned curriculum to incorporate the SCAA document, *Desirable Outcomes on Entering Compulsory Education*. The nursery introduced the children to a number of different experiences, including sand, water, paint, modelling, working on the computer, drawing, construction, reading and dressing up. The nursery curriculum covered language and literacy; mathematics; creative development; physical development; personal and social development; and knowledge and understanding of the world.

The nursery area consisted of one large room with an outside play area. Parts of the classroom were sectioned off – there was an area for hearing stories, a book corner and a place to work on computers. There was also a home corner and an interest table. The room was large and bright, and the drawings and models of the children were displayed on the walls. There were two staff; a (male) teacher and a (female) nursery nurse. They worked collaboratively to develop a supportive and friendly learning environment for the children. New themes tied into National Curriculum objectives were introduced every half term. Over the period of my observation, these themes included:

Our bodies Children painted themselves, made models of themselves, explored themselves through handprints and footprints, read stories about the body

Our environment Children visited the park, the shops, the local fire station, and drew and recorded their experiences

Shops and shopping This project is described in Chapter 3. It included making shopping bags, discussing shopping and going to a shop.

These different subjects were explored in a variety of ways. In addition to project work, the children were read to regularly every morning and again before going home. They collected information on letter sounds, and worked on particular letters. They were encouraged to write their own names. Numeracy was a key part of nursery work, and the children were encouraged to count out beads, bits of clay, buttons and fingers. Clay was used to project the concepts of half and smaller and larger. Another aspect to the curriculum was design and technology. The teachers gave the children opportunities to practise folding, layering, construction, and to observe differences in weight and mass. There was science and biology – children observed plants, and discussed the weather and the habitats of different animals. Learning was facilitated through planned trips as well as experiential discussions. Children brought in favourite toys and books from home to share, which added to the richness of the curriculum. The outside play area was a place to experience physical activities – using tricycles, slides and the hoops and tunnels to feel for themselves how shapes made a difference to play.

Learning was informal and supported by a wide variety of resources including books, a computer, paint, modelling materials and an outdoor space. Each day a planned activity would take place in the morning and afternoon with a group of children. On a day to day basis the teachers tried to keep a balance between child directed and adult directed tasks and activities by tracking the attendance of children at the key activities. During the period of my observation, the children made use of a wide variety of media, including clay, paint, glue, collage, string, masking tape, water, sand, chalk, gravel, paper, pens and glitter. This multi-media approach to learning is a characteristic and valuable part of nursery practice and it led to emphasising the multi-modal text in the observations.

I played a curious role in the nursery. Initially, I was simply, 'Barney's mum' – my son was in the nursery at that time. As the nature of the work unfolded, I became also the lady who liked to take things away. That I took a handbag and a camera in with me did not go unnoticed by the children. (See Chapter 3 for a discussion of the children's enthusiasm for making handbags and cameras.) I took notes and recorded what I saw as unobtrusively as possible, and retained an ambiguous position. I was a 'mummy' but also a 'helper' who came in to work with the children at the modelling table. By being part of the class yet not a teacher, I could become the children's friend. I did become friendly with some children, and they tended to give me their work. Being allowed to take work away was valuable for the research, although it was also interesting when children resisted my attempts to do so. The school welcomed me and was supportive to both my observation and my helping. My role as parent allowed me insights into the children's work which was different from the insights of, for example, a student. I could see what happened to certain work when it came home.

I did not have access to all the work in the nursery, however. Knowing no Bengali, Turkish or Somali denied me access to some of the conversations about models. I was not seen as part of those communities, and my role as 'Barney's mum' defined me as the parent of a white, middle class boy. Some things about me were ambiguous – was I a parent, a researcher or a helper? However, this position enabled the research to have a particular depth and a focus. I knew intimately the school I observed and the context of the practice. Much of this I received as a parent, at parents' evenings. As a researcher, my data was therefore richer but also more local, more subjective than the data of an outsider who had chosen the school at random. Mine was a selective study, in a pre-selected school. My enthusiasm for the project, for the school and for the children's work drove me on to develop the observation structure and the research.

Observation as a tool

By recording details of each session as closely as possible, I tried to achieve what the anthropologist Clifford Geertz called 'thick description' (Geertz 1973 p.6). In other words, everything the children did was regarded as significant and worthy of attention. Assuming that gesture, talk and play are all acts of significance, I tried to make notes of what I saw happening in all its complexity. I also tried to understand where the children got ideas for their work. I could watch the children hear stories, see them play in the home corner, and track their drawing and modelling activities. I was able to see how the teachers created a structure for the children which embraced different textures and modes and additionally developed early literacy activities. I watched how the children interacted with the curriculum. By observing closely what children actually did in a nursery, I was able to see how they formulated their ideas. I became immersed in the worlds of the children and their preoccupations, from Cruella De Vil to Spiderman, from car washes to princesses. I heard the stories they listened to when they first came in and settled down for their morning story. I moved with them to the 'making table' where they expressed their ideas through model making. During the first term of the observations my son attended the nursery, thus allowing me to watch what happened to his model making at home and at school. I took data from his early writing and model making to supplement the research project, but the main body of the research was conducted in the classroom with a group of three and a half to four year olds. Like an anthropologist, I was both of, and not of, this group of people. I learnt from watching them and began to formulate my ideas.

Observation as a tool is rich in possibilities. While we cannot probe the psyche, we can use techniques such as observation and analysis of the things children make to give us insights about how thought is structured, as well as how the social organisation of the world appears to the child. This possibility gives rise to several levels of insight. One can observe how a model is shaped and developed, and understand the model in terms of its construction. If it is a truck, for example, that meaning, as perceived by the child, is important. The model also has a history, which includes the child's previous experience of trucks and the encounters the child has had with them. The child may also have imbued the truck with certain emotional feelings – it may mean for its creator an enclosed space, a reminder of other important closed spaces. The making of the truck is shaped by the past but it is also shaped by the future. The truck has meaning in that it may be made for an audience – the peer group or the teacher or other important adults in the child's life. The truck may also have been created as part of a wider reflection on trucks. It may have been transposed to the model from another place where it had been discussed. The observer has to consider all these variables in the making of the truck, before the truck making can be situated within a wider perspective, namely the developing communication by the child.

However, even detailed observation is a partial tool. We are always informed by our own perceptions. It is never possible to understand fully what is going on inside children's minds as they are creating something. The influence of the observer's thoughts and ideas often supercedes the reality of the situation. The complexity of this process of watching other people is well expressed by Geertz (1973):

> Doing ethnography is like trying to read (in the sense of 'construct a meaning of') a manuscript – foreign, faded, full of ellipses, incoherencies, suspicious emendations, and tendentious commentaries, but written not in conventionalized sound but in transient examples of shaped behaviour. (p.10)

Parents and teachers as researchers

Teachers can track children's meaning making, and thereby develop the work still further. Here we have a model of teacher as researcher in the classroom. The space can enable teachers to create new ideas in the classroom and so 'make a difference' to the work they are already doing. By observing and tracking the model making of the children, they can add value to the already deep and complex work they are doing. In tracking children's literacy progress they can give depth to a child's language and literacy record and offer insights to parents. Parents can become partners in this process and, by observing and recording work done at home, meet teachers half way with their information. The project can become one of mutual exploration and support for the tracking process.

In *Threads of Thinking: young children learning and the role of early education* (1994) Cathy Nutbrown offered us the concept of 'schemas' to describe children's consistent patterns of behaviour. She suggested that parents and teachers should observe young children in order to find out what interests them, and then extend and develop the patterns or schemas that children are interested in. For example, a child who consistently uses the notion of 'inside and outside' in play, or one who is playing in circular motions, may be adopting that pattern of behaviour because they are interested in those concepts. Nutbrown's ideas can be developed into observing the communication patterns of children. The particular interests of children – layering for example – can be developed through collage or through putting things in boxes. To find out how children work, a record is needed of children's texts and also a way of interpreting them. There also needs to be a record of the context in which they were produced. This concept engages with the everyday items that children produce routinely. An investigation into children's work takes everything they produce as being meaningful, not just the more attractive products. These products are then put together to form a picture of each child's thoughts and ideas.

The next stage is to write a careful account of the process of producing each item, to include the teacher/researcher's comments on how he or she interpreted the work or the situation as it unfolded. By using these records, with the children's texts, a composite picture can be built up of *how* children are producing texts and *what* they are producing. The teacher can then enable more productive and interactive conversations with the children to move the work on still further. By keeping notes of modelling sessions and records of children's drawings, a profile can be built up of each child, and, indeed, a group of children. The work of the children can spawn new projects. It is generally the children who generate the narrative they are working within.

The process of observation can focus on the design of an object, and try to understand its relation to a page. Things like the child's decisions whether to cover a whole page or half a page; whether to cut something out, whether to cover with collage, are all of significance. The origin of a model can be understood in terms of where it comes from and also in terms of its shape, form and structure. A sign is made with intention, with meaning – but it also made within a space. This space offers certain resources. What the child does with these resources provides new meanings and new forms of representation.

The process of collecting the children's texts and then writing close observation is critical. By minutely studying a group of children and their texts, a composite picture can be built up. Taking account of the views and thoughts of the observer can offer a richer model of what is being modelled, which can then be followed up. If what children are engaged with is carefully observed, their work can be developed and supported within the classroom structure.

Studies of children's work

Many writers have observed children at work. Readers may be interested in books such as Michael Armstrong's *Closely Observed Children* (1980) which offered an analysis of how children create in the classroom, achieved through close description of children at work. Bussis and Chittenden's *Inquiry Into Meaning* (1985) used close description of children's reading and writing development combined with analysis of the children's drawing and the context in which their work was produced, to build up a detailed picture of how children come to read. The central argument of *Inquiry Into Meaning* was that personal meanings can be valid subject matter for educational research. This view informs the work of my study. In both, subjectivity is seen as part of the process of doing research. Subjective meanings, combined with close description and rigorous analysis of data, can offer deeper understandings of the complex work of creating that children are constantly engaged in.

Conclusion

While this chapter offers a 'way in' to observation of young children, the next chapter describes more closely the process by which ideas move from one medium to another. It is this process that this book is trying to track. The observation research was such that I was able to track ideas as they arose and were expressed by the children. I could then study the texts and understand the context in which they were produced. Subjecting texts to such a 'close reading' allowed a deeper understanding of their meaning and context to emerge. Parents and teachers, by giving full attention to children's work, can become more aware of what is happening when they draw or model. Activity that did not seem to have a focus can be valued and credited. By using our perception as a research tool, the child's world can be uncovered.

Chapter 3

Tracking the flow
Seeds, baskets and shopping

Observation 11th October 1996

There were shopping bags hung on the washing line... Lydia made a carpet initially, with pieces of felt. This was turned into a basket. They had been making baskets all week... Lucy made a shopping basket and then attached a notebook to it, which she wrote in. When she had finished she said, 'This was writing to show my mum'.

This chapter describes how the children I observed started working in one particular mode or form, and then moved across modes as their interest demanded. Objects tended to spawn new meanings as they were extended in modelling activities. One object would generate another. I explore the concept that one idea can be expressed in different forms: as a model, a drawing, play or talk. The links between listening to a story and modelling can be uncovered by watching children model. I stress the importance of listening to children's talk to understand how their making is put into context. When analysing children's work, it is important to recognise the influence of the media: videos, television and stories. I also explore the concept of internalisation – the way children reproduce the images from their own internal 'memory bank' of ideas. Children's modelling needs to be carefully watched. It is often different from what we suppose. Models may not be finished when we think they are. The **influence** behind the making of a model needs exploring.

Modelling was encouraged in the nursery. The teacher developed the idea of free modelling as he worked with the children, and parents were encouraged to bring in boxes and packets from home for the children.

The 'making table', as it was called, also held collage materials, glue and sticky tape, all readily available. The classroom was covered with the results of the children's work – free drawing, depictions of fire engines, shopping bags and snakes hanging on a washing line across the classroom, painting and writing.

The children were given explicit encouragement to draw, paint and model during the nursery sessions. Although many children chose to play outside on the bikes and climbing frame during nursery sessions, each session also provided one focus activity for the children to join in. The teachers made sure that each child participated in these activities over the term, and space was provided for children to engage in modelling activities. The teachers recognised that literacy and communication could be extended to a wide variety of activities, including modelling, drawing and play. The structure was loose and allowed children to control the content and form of their work.

What interested me in the observations were firstly the links between objects and activities and then the objects that grew from these activities. Tracking the flow of ideas from books, to internal thoughts, to new objects and then further objects was a key part of the observation process. For example, as part of a project on shopping, the children were making seed trays out of egg boxes. These things began to be linked together in the children's minds. A child might begin to make a shopping basket, and then add a few seeds at the bottom to create a seed basket. These links drove the children on to investigate other possibilities. Seed baskets became shopping baskets. These then grew shopping lists. A group of ideas in the mind was expressed as a transforming series of objects. The objects changed meaning as they were being developed.

Coming into the nursery one day, I noticed shopping bags hanging on a line going right across the nursery. One bag had been written on – the word was 'Sainsbury's'. The picture on the bag was a bright and sunny smiling face (See Figure 3.1).

The teacher explained that as part of the curriculum the children had been doing a project on 'shopping'. Parents were encouraged to bring in discarded remnants of shopping – egg boxes, loo roll insides, old plastic bottles and cardboard boxes. These were used at the modelling table but they also stimulated the children's thinking. The children also listened to stories, such as Eric Carle's *The Tiny Seed*. Much of what I observed lay within this group of ideas of seeds, growing, food, shopping.

Figure 3.1

When I sat down at the modelling table, I was fascinated by Lydia making what she told me was to be a carpet, with pieces of felt. She then selected a container which she described as a basket. At the bottom of the basket she placed the collection of felt squares. The carpet had been transformed and was now a basket with a soft covering at the bottom (See Figure 3.2).

Where did Lydia's carpet/basket come from? The carpet may have come from a home story or dolls' house. The basket theme had come from school, partly because baskets were popular with the children, and partly from the current shopping theme. The felt squares were 'planted' at the bottom of the basket as if they would grow.

Another project initiated in the nursery was the seed box made from egg boxes and dried pulses. The children were encouraged to fill egg boxes with dried pulses and glue them inside, so that the seeds could be said to have been 'planted'. These were then taken home. The carpet/basket expressed the number of different themes Lydia was exploring at the time – baskets, carpets and seeds, all in one object. It was as if she had put a number of different structures together. This for me was an indica-

Figure 3.2

tion of the way her mind was internally 'gluing together' different concepts. The basket expressed a number of different ideas at the same time. Why the connection between basket and carpet? I was interested in this since the object created more questions: did this 'carpet' emanate from the idea of a seed box producing a 'carpet' of grass, or was the word association more vague?

I started by looking at where things came from. When my own child, Barney, who was still in the nursery at the time, brought home a seed box and put it in the window sill I realised that objects carried on creating meaning outside the space of the nursery (See Figure 3.3).

Part of my research concerned what happened to objects when they were taken home. In the case of the seed tray, the object generated its own new set of ideas – outside of the nursery space. Barney had been reading *The Tiny Seed*. He much enjoyed the story, perhaps because it suggested that small people (children) could become large and significant (the seed becomes a flower). Barney took his seed box home, laid it on the windowsill, and expected the seeds to grow. From this came his question, 'Where was I before I was a tiny seed, Mummy?' For him the project had become translated into looking at origins and at how things became other things.

I watched Lucy make a shopping basket out of an old tissue box. She carefully made a handle for it. Then she wrote out a list, which she attached to the basket with a piece of tape. When I asked her what the writing was, she said that it was 'writing to show my mum' (See Figure 3.4).

By linking the list to the basket, Lucy had made the connection between going shopping and making a list. She had developed the linguistic concept of list + basket into the object. As with Lydia's basket, several concepts – shopping, basket and list – had been put together into one object. The things that are linked in the mind have become linked in the material world. Within the minds of the children we can track the beginnings of word association; from seeds and carpets to baskets. At certain points, the concrete reality of the sculptures expresses this word association. Using one idea, the children are driven by internal links within them to explore other possibilities. This reflects both the children's inner thoughts and their interest in how the object looks. Both impulses are at work. If an object reminds children of something else, they are able to develop it structurally so that it becomes the thing inside their heads. The meanings change and grow inside their minds. These meanings then

Figure 3.3

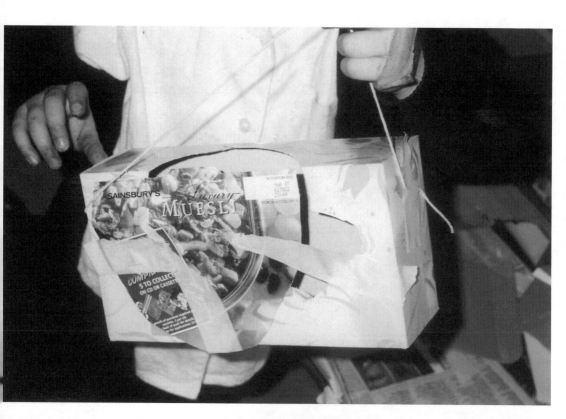

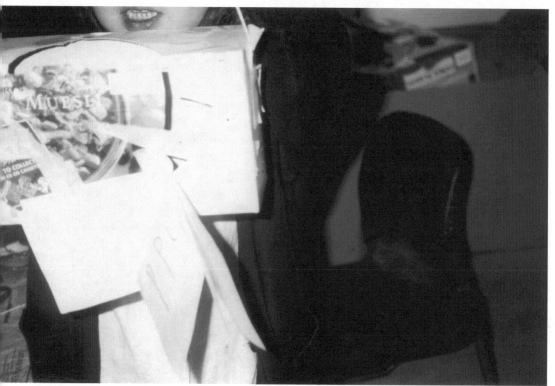

Figure 3.4

develop as they move from one concept to another. They are also revealed when children make an object. I was initially surprised at how often a child apparently finished one object, and then transformed it into something else. I could not understand why until I worked out the associations going on inside the child's mind. Often a child would link objects both internally and externally. It was one of my tasks as researcher to uncover these links. While they were often displayed on the surface of the text the children produced, they also sometimes referred to deep structures within the their minds. A list always goes with shopping, so why not attach a list to a shopping basket? By actually gluing two separate items together, the children were showing how in our minds we link the two together.

These objects had a fluid quality: they appeared to be finished and then the children would revise them. Many of my observations questioned the concept of the finished object. Many teachers' idea of model making is that it is contained within the space of the nursery 'two hour' time slots. However, models would be made, revised at home, and then return to the nursery in a different form. The adult constrictions of: 'it's tidy up time, now we must finish' often did not apply to the children's work. What the teachers were unable to track was what happened to the models when they were taken home.

By tracking what the children read and take in, and what they subsequently produce in a variety of modes, it becomes possible to understand more about how they see the world and how they develop ideas. Looking closely at what children do reveals how they can express complex ideas in a material form, without the need for access to written modes of expression. For the children, models are part of a wider process of thought and developing ideas, and the production of a model is a point of reflection for them, a way of meditating on an idea and then pushing it further.

Gunther Kress has highlighted this movement across different modes:

> the successive transitions from one mode of representation to another – from drawing; to coloured-in, labelled drawing; to cut-out object; to the object integrated into a system of other objects, changing its potential of action; from one kind of realism to another; from one form of imaginative effort to another – these seem to me what humans do and need to do, and need to be encouraged to do as an entirely ordinary and necessary part of human development, (Kress 1997 p.29)

These transitions 'from one kind of realism to another' are particularly interesting when we look at the work of young children. The separation between the child's mind and the outside world is not yet complete, so that a seed box or a basket could both symbolise an internal state, and come to life on a window sill. Things have a quality of realism for children which adults may have learnt is not possible. The world is full of growing seeds, babies who came from a seed, and baskets that sprout shopping. Objects such as seed boxes lie on the interface of being a representation and being a 'real thing'. Model making and the third dimension can be seen as a window into the real world; animation brings them 'to life'. By using many objects that suggest 'new life' – seeds, baskets, egg boxes, little womb-like objects – the children seem to be directly addressing issues of animation and, perhaps, questions of identity.

Making media

I also watched children employing concepts taken from their experience of stories and the media to develop new objects. Joe made a robot ugly duckling and then developed Spiderman from the first structure (see Figure 3.5).

The origins of these objects are as follows. The children had been reading the story *The Ugly Duckling*. In Joe's version this creature has a beak and wings. However, it has an automated aspect and can be seen to be in the process of becoming a robot. Joe was, I think, initially interested in the idea of the ugly duckling. When he finished making it, it looked to him like a robot. A more plausible explanation for its shape, which had a sword-like protrusion added, was a Spiderman. Joe took an idea from a traditional fairy tale and from cartoons on television to make his object, illustrating how children's productions are a mix of different ideas and influences that they then put together to form objects which are entirely new.

Here, the object had gone through a series of transformations. It had followed the flow of Joe's thought processes and his focus on the object's shape. The objects had echoes of a number of narratives that turn on transformation for their meaning, including *The Ugly Duckling*, Spiderman and possibly the science fiction/Dr Who narratives involving robots. Many of the boys in the nursery were preoccupied with narratives such as Power Rangers and Batman. In later observations, I could see how these interests led many children, particularly boys, to want to transform themselves and turn into something else. Such is the power for the children of the idea of a shape-shifter.

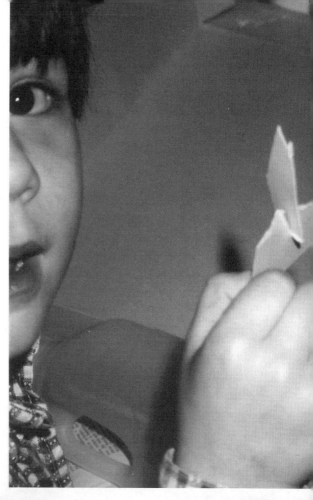

Figure 3.5

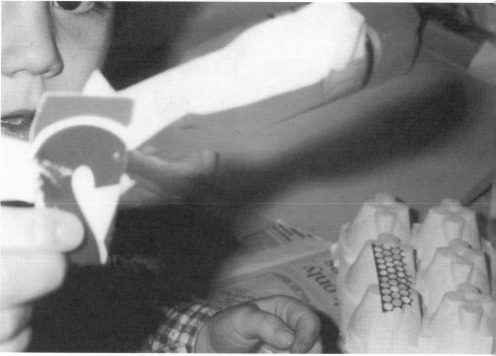

The nursery created the seeds of ideas and the children transformed them into new objects. The inside of toilet rolls for example, regularly provided by parents, and part of the vocabulary of the nursery children's sign making. Like the baskets, they were routine objects about the nursery, used for a variety of purposes, and slipping in their usage from one meaningful structure to another. One might be fitted onto a child's hand to make Captain Hook's hook. The 'claw' was made from cardboard, and the join achieved with masking tape (Figure 3.6).

Using the observation records to trace the Captain Hook theme shows how various children were captivated by the story of *Peter Pan* (available in the nursery to read). As well as his hook, children made versions of Captain Hook's hat, and one child wanted to make Tinkerbell's wings. Part of the reason for making these objects was that the materials were available for them to do so. The children's interest, evoked by a story they had heard, interacted with the creative nursery environment to produce new structures.

Figure 3.6

The transforming sign

Tracking the processes of meaning making as new signs were created was fascinating. Children would seize on one idea – say the seed basket – and quietly work at a model. This model would reflect how the idea had moved and shifted in the child's mind. The influence of meaningful narratives, thoughts and feelings ('Where was I before I was a seed?') pushed ideas forward so that new structures could be created. By observing this over time, it is possible to establish where ideas came from, track them through a series of different incarnations, and then note how they become incorporated into model making and narrative play. Within a few weeks in this particular nursery the following influences were evident:

> *Peter Pan*
> *Cinderella*
> Spiderman
> *The Ugly Duckling*
> *The Tiny Seed*
> Sainsbury's/shopping
> The park
> *The Rainbow Fish*
> Carpet at home
> Me/self
> Parents
> Teacher

As different children used this combination of influences in their model making a pattern built up. These are just the few influences I was able to observe – a more detailed observation would pick out hundreds of stories, experiences, people and places that make up a child's inner world. The play and talk in the class developed the influences. Stories such as *The Ugly Duckling*, *The Tiny Seed*, *The Rainbow Fish* and *Peter Pan* were developed in play situations and then moved into drawing and models. Children could take on a number of roles within a story. A variety of different models could be made from one story, for example, *Peter Pan* generated a hook, a hat and a pair of wings. *The Ugly Duckling* could become a robot and then transmute into Spiderman. Narratives could mix, like two different colours in a thread of wool, and become something new and different.

Sometimes ideas would surface in different modes, a process which Kress (1997) has described as translation or **transduction**. The idea becomes translated, much as a concept is translated into a different language.

However, in each mode the sign is slightly different and might reflect different aspects of the thing described. A seed drawn on a piece of paper has less potential as a seed than a dried pea in an egg box. Children's desire to develop new signs and to transform existing signs is evidence of their specific interest in form and function.

Symbol making

Many of the objects the children made had a symbolic aspect in that they were imbued with wider meanings. Like play and drawing, model making can be seen to be a symbolising activity which harnesses children's thoughts and feelings. By a symbol, I mean the way in which ideas and emotions are transferred to outside objects. Things 'stand for' certain emotions and feelings. For example, these powerful models of seeds and baskets can be read as the children's attempts to use symbols to explore questions of origin and identity. By talking to children about their work, and by tracking the process of making, I realised how many of the objects meant more to the children than merely the things they were supposed to be. Consequently, the object could then be developed in another mode.

The influence of the group

The ideas and work of their peer group were among the most important influences on the children. Time and again I would see a child make something which would be seized on and copied by the rest of the children round the table. Children used these structures in their own ways. Objects were often generated within the group, and had their own logic. The nursery would be obsessed with making bracelets or making princesses or masks, and these objects acquired their own momentum. Group processes amongst the children contributed to this spread of concepts, with the result that concepts were constantly changing.

The change process was shaped in two ways. It could depend upon how each child interacted individually with other children – if for example, two children had a special relationship which meant that they would often work together. Girls often worked together on a collaborative basis – but not always. At other times an object would be of significance to a wider group of children, and the object itself would take over. Everyone would want to make a mask or a bracelet. This is another aspect of group processes at work – the way in which ideas would catch on and become popular. The tighter group processes may dictate smaller, more similar object making or drawing, but even in such cases, I noticed huge differences in how each child interpreted, for example, a princess. The internal concepts laid down in children's minds seemed to create diverse patterns within an overall pattern of things that are popular and habitual.

The researcher as generator of data

Influences from outside – peers, teachers, researchers – often dictated what was being made. Having a researcher in the classroom also had an effect. My very presence changed the objects made in the nursery. Because I brought a camera in to the classroom, one child made a camera from an empty plastic bottle – and pointed it at me (See Figure 3:7).

I was accustomed to photographing the children; now they were to photograph me. And many of the children made handbags, into which they would put things. I, of course, took a handbag into the classroom, and at the end of the session would collect things to put into it.

Figure 3.7

Concept formation

Through watching children's ideas unfold it is possible to discover the child's formation of concepts. A concept could arise in a child's mind and then be tried out in play or in a drawing. To the child, this is the first step in making the object real in the external world. We can call this process **externalisation**. The child can externalise a thought through a drawing or model. For example, Joe's Spiderman Ugly Duckling was a product of his thought processes. Joe had put the two thoughts together in his mind, and then revealed this gluing together by his model. Likewise, Lucy put her shopping list and basket together in her model because in her mind the two belonged together.

Ideas can also be **internalised**: a child can listen to a story and then internalise it. The narrative enters the realm of 'inner speech', the concept of which comes from Vygotsky's chapter, Thought and Word (1986). Inner speech can then be translated into outer speech. For example, for Barney, hearing the story *The Tiny Seed* led to thoughts about seeds and about growing. He took on the concept and made a seed box, which he brought home and placed on the windowsill. A new sign, the egg box, had been created with the potential to grow. From the initial hearing of the story, to the creation of the egg box with seeds in it, there had been a process of internalising the idea, thinking about it, and then externalising it in the form of the egg box. The developing of the new idea had been expressed in the model so it can be linked to the concept of 'inner speech' – which is quite difficult to observe. Sometimes children at play will talk to themselves in an interior monologue. Some drawings, particularly those done at home, capture this quality.

The model described above also helps us to analyse the 'unfinished' nature of some of the objects. While they may have started out as one object, we can see how they develop into another. Just as ideas in the mind rise and follow a train of thought and then run off in another direction, so did these children's models follow lines of inquiry, and were stages in thought processes that were sometimes, and sometimes not, completed.

Some objects are more clearly derived from traces of internal structures whereas others are formulated so that we cannot uncover their traces. However, many of the objects I observed being made in the nursery seemed to belong to the area between the child's 'inner speech' and the external world. The objects were being made in a space away from the eye of the teacher, and my presence was silent, non-participatory. The other explanation is that many objects were destined for the home, and lay outside the realm of school. The home/school divide, I would argue, informs the context and the substance of what children make. This may be an unconscious motivating factor, but my observation is that things arise in a slightly different form at home and at school. 'Inner speech' is more possible at home.

'Inner speech' describes an area which lies between the child and the outside world. The place where many of the children's drawings took place belonged neither to the external world nor to the inner workings of the mind. Donald Winnicott (1971 p.3) describes this area 'the realm of experiencing'. The area is to be found where there is a gap between 'me' and 'not me'. In the early stages of children's development, the 'transitional object' bridges that gap. Winnicott describes children's passion for a 'transitional object' such as a teddy bear, which acts as a causeway between the child's mother and the outside world. The teddy bear 'stands for' or symbolises the mother and at the same time 'stands for' and symbolises the outside world. Symbolism as 'standing for' something else is an important part of children's internal signs. Many of the children's models were expressions of their inner world.

This analysis indicates that many of children's drawings and models, like 'inner speech', are a way of being. Often drawn in a safe space, they are a sign of children's concept formation in the making. They are newly made signs, indicating the shifting territory between the internal space and the external world.

By watching this process minutely the origin of concept formation can be identified. It becomes possible to talk about a landscape of representation. This is motivated by a series of complex impulses, and expresses itself in a variety of forms. This landscape is constantly shifting, and moves in and out of internal and external spaces. Uncovering this landscape reveals how ideas can be expressed in a material form, without the need to have access to written modes of expression. The work is not only being developed in a purely linguistic terrain but it also embraces a much wider communicational landscape encompassing space, surface, colour, shape, line and texture.

Implications for practice in nursery classrooms

- **The multi-modal text**
  When developing a project in the nursery, for example on 'my body', it is often beneficial to explore the concept in a number of different modes – such as drawing a child's body on the floor, making a model of a body, and drawing faces and shapes. This allows children to express different ideas in different forms.

- **Making links**
  Making links between what the children are reading and what they are modelling can be helpful because it allows children to see where their model is situated. Ideas can then be traced back and forth between different modes.

- **Listening to children**
  Listening to children's talk while they are making models may provide clues to where the model comes from. This can be taken full circle – from story to model and then back to story, with some diversions on the way.

- **The influence of the media**
  The media and videos are important in tracking the ideas behind models. Often children articulate ideas beyond the nursery sphere and bring their home experiences into their work. This needs to be acknowledged.

- **Home and school**
  Children's internal thoughts and internal talk may be expressed obliquely through the models they make. What is articulated at home is also important. Teachers need to be sensitive to the relationship between the home and school in generating models and be aware that models made at home may have deep significance for the child. Children should be allowed to take models home with them when they want to.

- **The developing object**
  Teachers need to be aware of the concept of the 'developing object' and to understand that objects are fluid and may not be finished until the child decides they are.

- **Tracking the flow**
  A chart can be made, as in the list above, of children's influences and events generated by nursery projects. Objects the children make can then be chronologically plotted on this chart to reveal how each child is responding to particular influences.

The way in which children's minds generate ideas and cross boundaries of form and structure has been described in this chapter in terms of what children actually produce. By thus observing the productive powers of children we can understand how children have the ability to transform their environment and make new signs. Introducing opportunities for model making and developing ideas extends and challenges children. When teachers decide in advance what the children are to make when doing modelling with them, they are closing off modelling possibilities. A dynamic classroom would incorporate children's developing ideas across its walls, taking account of their home lives and their interests. Perhaps this would produce a less 'ordered' display, but the gain would be to uncover the powerful undercurrents that lie behind the productions children make.

Chapter 4

The third dimension
Making things more real

Observation 26/11/96

Abigail started to cut out a fish. 'It's a rainbow fish – from my Dad's computer'. She coloured it in carefully with stripes. Then she cut out two side bits, one white, one yellow. We discussed the fins, and she said that they were like wings, to push the fish along. The teacher drew a fish and she cut it out and coloured it in. Then she asked for some paper to mount her fishes on. I photographed the fish, and then the two fish mounted. This took about an hour.

The last chapter looked at how children generated the objects they made; this one concentrates on children's choice of a form for their object and explores why the move into the third dimension was significant for the children. It then goes on to discuss children and their bodies and how they brought them into their model making. Space and its significance in the classroom is considered, since the third dimension widens to include everything around the children. We examine how three dimensional work was included in the children's play, and how many activities were generated by the props the children had made at the making table. The chapter ends by showing how early literacy activities can be experienced as three dimensional, and suggesting ways of developing early literacy from work that children develop in the third dimension.

Watching the children convinced me that the decision to move from drawing to modelling was often significant. They used the possibilities of the third dimension for a reason – mostly when they wanted to make something 'more real'. For example, I watched Zainab draw and then cut out a penguin. Then she wanted to use cut out black paper for the eyes. Zainab gave the penguin an added boost of realism by placing two pieces of black paper on either side of it, so moving the work into the third dimension.

To facilitate communicating about signs, I would like to suggest a theoretical 'way in' to describing what the children are making. It uses the ideas of Michael Halliday, who describes signs in terms of three over-arching functions or metafunctions.

Halliday's three metafunctions

Halliday (1979) suggests that in communicating and in representing our-selves to the world we always do three things. Firstly, we say something about the world through the object – he calls this the **ideational** function of the sign. Secondly, we say something about the relationships that object has with the world – he calls this the **interpersonal** function of the sign. Thirdly, we say something about the sign's form and composition as we make the sign – this is the **textual** function. A child's model can be described in terms of what it represents, how it is represented, and the social setting in which it is produced. This gives us a language in which to talk about the things the children made.

If we take Lucy's shopping basket (see Figure 3.4), the **ideational** aspect of the sign is its manifestation as a shopping basket and list. This is the content of the sign which, in this case, came from the shopping project in the nursery. The **interpersonal** aspect is its relationship with the outside world – in Lucy's case, as she said while making it, 'This is for my mummy.' The object also communicates Lucy's relationship with the shopping project. She had listened to the shopping stories and been on shopping trips. This is her attempt to communicate her experience of shopping to the outside world. In terms of the **textual** function of the sign, we can analyse its form. It is made out of a tissue box, with an opening cut at one end. Masking tape has been used to attach another piece of cardboard over the opening at the side so that the basket is closed. Masking tape is also used to attach a piece of string to the box for a handle. In the second picture, the basket has a list attached to it, with some writing on it in green.

When children are making an object, the ideational, interpersonal and textual are all at play. Children may initially be driven by the content, and may need to tell a story, such as: Here am I going shopping with a basket. They may also be considering who should be the audience for the product. In this case it was the child's mother. The object's design was changed to respond to the childs' view of her mother's needs – she needs a list before she goes shopping – so a list was attached. Finally, there are decisions to be made about how big the object is to be, how much colour to put on it, how much to cut out and how much to leave.

The importance of the move from 2 D to 3 D – one example

Here is an example of a child working in the second dimension and then moving to working in three dimensions. It demonstrates the changing shape and meaning of the model as it progresses through this process. By focusing carefully on this one example, we can understand the importance of the shape and function of the sign to create the meaning.

In this case, I was at the making table when Abigail came to do some work and started to cut out a fish. As she worked, she commented: 'It's a rainbow fish – from my Dad's computer'. She coloured it in carefully, giving it stripes. She cut out two side bits, one white and one yellow. We discussed the fins, and she said that they were like wings, to push the fish along. She asked for another fish to be made, and the teacher drew a fish. She cut the fish out and coloured it in. Finally she asked for some paper to mount her fishes on. She carefully mounted the two fishes on a white background, and coloured in some sea around them (See Figure 4.1).

Abigail's fishes were an exploration of the process of moving from 2D to 3D. First she cut out and coloured in the fish. The 'side bits' – fins – were placed so that they stuck out at either side, so the fish floated in space. But Abigail was not satisfied with this. A second fish was made, so that the fish became 'two fish' and the whole was mounted onto white card, with a coloured sea in around them. The fish was once more in an environment, put within the display.

Abigail's initial motivation was drawn from the 'rainbow fish' on her father's computer. A conversation with her mother revealed that there were fishes on its 'screen saver'. Abigail could also have been influenced by a story at school about a rainbow fish. This was the ideational function of the sign, the content. Abigail was also keen to tell the teacher about her rainbow fish – she wanted to convey a message when making the fish that 'here is my fish, I know about this'. This was the interpersonal function of the sign – about the relationship between the sender of the sign and the outside world. However, her desire to do this was overtaken by her interest in the fish, and then its relation to the second fish, and its own environment, the sea. This was the textual aspect of the sign. The textual possibilities of a fish, two fishes, sea and then display were exploited to the full. Abigail's fish had moved through different

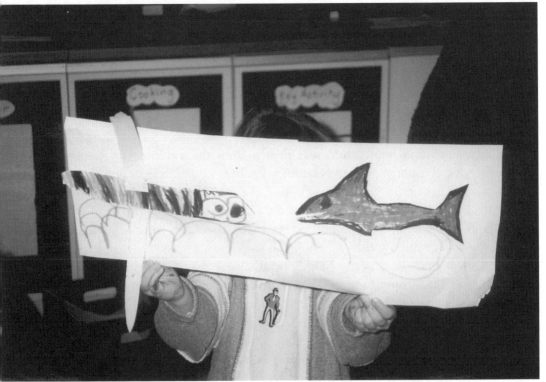

Figure 4.1

modes to end up not a lone fish in a nursery sea, but a fish in a white sea coloured in with blue. A form of transformation had occurred.

During the whole process of making the model Abigail had been interested in the process itself. She was led by the design or shape of the fish she was making to explore further possibilities. Her primary interest when making the fish was the shape it created. The final version – two fishes with fins in a white sea – was but one version of the fish. Each stage had its own integrity and interest. The meaning of the fish on its own shifted to the fish with another fish through the process of model making. In that process, the fish was 'cut-out', 'animated' and eventually put back into the sea with the other fish.

Cutting out and animation

The process of cutting out offered profound opportunities for the children to lift their work into a different environment.

Gunther Kress's point is that:

> Cutting out may offer the child one means of bridging a gap between two kinds of imaginative worlds, one in which the child 'enters the page' so to speak, and imaginatively enters into the life of objects or on the page; and another in which represented objects come off the page and are brought into the world of physical objects here and now, which are then re-animated in the imaginative effort of the child. There is then a continuum for the child, between things on the page – one kind of distanced intangible reality; and things here and now, another kind of reality, not distanced but tangible. The two kinds of realism are linked through the actions of the child (Kress 1997, p.27).

The children in this nursery cut out, among other things, snakes, fishes, caterpillars, masks and people (See Figure 4.2).

The picture shows, for example, a 'cut out' caterpillar and two fishes. A form of animation governed this choice; as Gunther Kress describes, cutting out could be seen to be a form of re-animation, a way of placing an object (fish, snake, caterpillar or person) in the world. The act of cutting out makes an object three-dimensional and therefore 'real'. The significance of working in three dimensions could be that it provides a way for children to give objects their own external reality.

Animation is a profound human interest. By animation I mean the process of becoming something else – which can be a sort of commentary on

Figure 4.2

the real forms of everyday life. The children commented on their world through the use of props and costume to enhance their own sense of reality. For example, one day I came in to find the children seized with the idea of making binoculars. Part of the children's interest in this was to be able to 'see more clearly'. The children were transformed by their binoculars into hunters, bird watchers and star-gazers.

In the same way, children could become animals and turn into other kinds of objects through the use of three-dimensional design. Some of this was inscribed on the body. The nursery children turned themselves into other beings – penguins, robots, and princesses – by putting on disguises. They also transformed the objects they worked with so that they could be seen as 'the thing itself'. They were investigating the borders of realism. There was a constant slipping in and out of reality in the nursery. Plates of food could look edible. Seed boxes were made to contain real seeds. Sometimes children made life-size models.

A tension existed between the 'real' world of the home and the 'constructed' world of the nursery. Although the nursery seemed like home, with a 'home corner', the interesting experience of 'dinner time', and toilets and other home-type activities, the children were aware that this was not their home, and objects were often seen as different when produced in or taken to the home context. Some of the most important objects I witnessed being made were swiftly taken home. The nursery staff were not allowed to keep them. And I was not allowed to take Abigail's fish home – it was her fish, and it retained its independence from me and from the classroom by being carried off home.

The enabling space

Observation 13th September 1996

When I arrived the teacher had a big box and said he would be making things out of boxes. Lucy was making things out of straws. I sat at the drawing table and Abigail did a picture, made up of disassociated objects. One large one was of her mummy (with a big tummy). Some children were playing with boxes. One child lay in a box during the entire session. When I went back to the drawing table some boys were drawing roughly: Jack drew a person, and Joseph drew a tree, a branch and a stone.

Reflection on observation of 12th November 1996

I reflected on what nursery must feel like to the children. There were times when children were not getting attention and had to deal with this in some way. I am sometimes needed for this purpose. Drawing is a way of being in something, becoming safe in the drawing. Children such as Mutahhara and Barney retreat into drawing as a 'safe space'. The tracing exercise proved popular because the children could become safe in the drawing space.

We seldom consider how children experience the spaces they are expected to inhabit. Children of three and a half rarely make choices about the layout of the classroom, or decide which activity is most important. However, through watching their progress through a morning session, I was able to see that space was very important to the children. They inhabited the space they were in as if the way they inhabited it had meaning. In other words, they used the space constructively as a form of expression. Take my observation: that 'one child lay in a box during the entire session'. This child was using the box to express his need for safety. Another child wanted things 'very small' – another meaningful statement. Space and size are important to children, whose body shape is changing as they move through the nursery experience. By the time they arrive at Reception they will, quite literally, be bigger.

To create successfully, children need a space in which they can feel safe. As this creation so clearly contributes to the child's sense of safety, the provision of a safe space is a vital part of good nursery practice. When children are enabled to feel comfortable within the nursery space, every other form of learning can take place.

The meaningful space

The importance of space and shape and the interweaving of narrative were revealed everywhere in the nursery. In some cases, gesture and dance were also part of children's sign making. Everything the children did – whether dancing, singing, playing, fighting, drawing or making models – was of significance. Children could work in one medium, and then answer each other in another. Sometimes two different mediums were in dialogue with one another. A particular way of playing could be answered by the making of a sword, for example. Here are some examples from my observation notes:

Observation (27/9/96):

1 *Two girls wandered off and were dancing together – I sat with them and did some drawing. Lucy was very keen to work on her model of an ice cream, made with straws and bits of material. She asked for sellotape so she could tape together the bits of material. She told me the flavours of the ice-cream. She spent a long time over it, and was proud of the result.*

2 *Barney, Becky, Lucy and Lydia all began work at the making table. The teacher had laid out plastic straws, glue, bits of material, and lots of boxes – egg boxes and packets for tea etc. Each child took a box and began to decorate it. Barney embellished an egg box and put seeds in the bottom. He said it was a garden. Lydia did something with another box. Lucy took the inside of a toilet roll and began to put shapes on to it. Becky was immersed in sticking layers and layers of material on mountains of glue.*

Observation (26/11/96)

3 *The nursery class is becoming increasingly fascinated with putting things on themselves, whether hats, masks or masking tape. Barney mentioned a dressing-up session where he watched Lydia dress up – 'I wanted to marry her', he said.*

In the first example, I note the dancing of the children, and the almost simultaneous production of the ice-cream. The child who produced the ice cream could have been commenting on the dancing, or vice versa. Often models were made in response to other activities in the nursery. Outside influences were also evident – for example, dancing was associated with ice-cream, parties and being happy.

In example 2, the making of the seed boxes has generated the urge to create layered collage. The children did not describe these 'mountains of paper'; they simply responded to the material they were given. Often collage and modelling were initiated by the children in a spirit of 'let's see what this will turn into'. Layering, for the child who was doing it, was important in itself; she felt safe doing it over and over again. This was a child who was new to the nursery and needed to feel safe, so for her the layering was an important 'schema' or pattern of behaviour. It was her form of expression in the nursery.

Watching the children in the nursery, it was clear that space has a meaning for children. Example 3 shows how the children created a space where they could become other people. It was when the nursery children felt safe enough that they could engage in role-play. By dressing up, they were expressing further ideas about their relationships with each other. Barney was able to express his feelings for Lydia when watching her dress up. The dressing-up box was a focus for many of the children and they used it when they needed other identities to supplement their play.

The children also used space in a motivated way. The spaces they inhabited mattered to them. They knew the layout of the nursery intimately, observed this space and used it constructively. This was particularly true of the making table. The plethora of egg boxes, insides of toilet rolls, cereal packets and bottles clearly provided a means for the children to comment on space. They also made comments about their everyday lives – 'we went to the car wash,' for example. This could be related to the stories they were experiencing, so enabling them to link the form and the content in a way that was satisfying to them.

Children expressed their awareness of form and shape not only in their model making but also in their use of space within the nursery and for their own physical shapes. Deep and unconscious feelings were involved in the children's use of space. Many of their drawings reflected an interest in enclosed circles, and they worked with circles as a beginning point for their model making. For example, watch making, mask making, crown making, making flowers and suns all required circular shapes and were common features of nursery work.

Jack's drawing of 'space' for example, reveals his interest in the circular enclosing shape. Within that shape there are enclosing forms which bring to mind a child in the mother's womb. For Jack, however, the meaning is different: this is 'space' out there – the world of rockets and stars and the moon (Figure 4.3).

Bodies and space

The emphasis on 3D in the nursery meant that it was a readily available form of expression. It became an extension of the self. If children needed reassurance or wanted to 'feel big' they would ask me to help them produce life-size models. For example, after Zainab had produced the 'cut out' penguin described at the beginning of this chapter, she asked me to make a 'Zainab sized' penguin so that she could wear it as a penguin suit (See Figure 4.4).

Figure 4.3

Things that were cut to fit the children's bodies became all-powerful talismans. Several of the boys came to the nursery dressed as Batman, and this form of body adornment or shape shifting was clearly a preoccupation. One child spent a morning making Cruella de Vil's cloak, and then walked around wearing it with an air of invincible power (See Figure 4.5).

The animating power of 'cutting out' as described by Kress is relevant here, as is the use of costume to enhance reality and develop play structures. Children can make a costume and with it transform the relationship they have with the surrounding space. Change is thus achieved through cutting out and sticking.

Conversely, children were also interested in the minute details of model making. At the making table, I noticed that some children opted for very

Figure 4.4

small pieces of paper. For some children collage appeared to be a way of being safe, going back to the womb. I watched one child repeatedly cover the same piece of cloth with more and more strips of felt. Layering a basket with strips of felt evidently created a safe space.

This preoccupation with space and the body extended into all areas of the nursery work. The body was the site on which things were modelled – masks, suits of armour, penguins and cloaks. The children's fingers were where letters were formed and on which numbers were counted. Feet were used to draw around, to map the contours of the classroom by running round the tables and chairs. The playground was another important space for many children, particularly the boys. On rainy days the frustration was evident, as the indoor space could scarcely contain their energies. Children often drew the playground, or walks they had

Figure 4.5

been on, as a natural extension of their experience of movement through time and space. To many of them, narrative literally meant a physical journey from one place to another. A small exploration round a new garden could yield a new shape or curve in the next drawing. The passage of time could be described by a wiggly line on a page. Space and time could be expressed in a two-dimensional medium. Drawing and map making could harness the power of play.

Mask making was an obvious activity that united the physical body and the child, and created transformation. It was extremely popular in the nursery at one point and the activity became extended in a number of ways. One morning when I was sitting at the making table, mask making took off. First Joe made a mask. Abdul began to make one, and so did Ziyaad. Mask making became frenetic. The masks had to be cut out, the

Figure 4.6

eyes cut away and string attached. I had to help cut out the eyes of some of them. Mask making became a focused activity, and the children wore their creations in the nursery. Mask making is an example of children using the third dimension to transform their bodies and 'animate' their faces into something different. Such transformations could be extended to the body, as with Zainab's penguin or Georgia's cloak.

At one time I noticed that the children in the nursery were becoming increasingly fascinated with putting things on themselves, whether hats, masks or masking tape. One day when I came in, some of the boys had been covering their bodies with armour. The masking tape began on the modelling table and ended up being used on the children as if they too were models, part of the 'play' they were engaged in. For example, Georgia used masking tape to create false eyelashes which she wore as decoration (See Figure 4.6).

The body had become a page to put things on or in. The children's familiarity with the classroom had extended to allow them to use their own bodies as decorative objects. The teacher's only comment when I noticed that one boy's upper body was covered in masking tape was: 'Yes, we're very keen on masking tape at the moment, aren't we?'

Play and props

Many of the models the children made, such as swords, crowns and masks, were used as props in dramatic play. Children would come to make their item – a watch, a pair of binoculars, a camera, a sword or a crown – and then walk into the outside play space to use their new prop. Some items, like the binoculars, gave their wearer new powers. Seeing became different and more powerful. Many of the boys asked for items that rendered them more powerful. Some of the girls favoured making things that led to a new role – such as Cruella de Vil or a Vamp figure. Much of the model making, once established, had this purposeful aspect. The use of the third dimension added realism to dramatic play. Models on the body were forms of dressing up and enabled the wearers to feel 'more real' in the roles they were adopting. The drive to change status linked ideas to models and then to play and talk. With masking tape and cardboard the children could transform their exterior selves at will and return to the group changed and empowered.

In another observation I watched the children making crowns, some of which were modified to become a *chador* or a mask. Boys made a 'transformers' mask and used them to initiate and develop play activities. They made watches to go with these outfits, which they used to 'slay' me. The children were also keen to make badges for favoured friends and family. Adorning the body with bits of cardboard became a preoccupation, manifest in the sudden interest in making false eyelashes, which were used to enhance the child's feeling of glamour and power. Many of the girls used props such as painted nails, false eyelashes, crowns or high heels to transform themselves into 'grown-up ladies'. These props were used as markers for different and powerful identities.

Literacy in the third dimension

Modelling also provided an opportunity to develop literacy skills – as in the case of Lucy's shopping basket and list. She wrote the list in 'pretend writing' and asked me for some significant letters. Her observation of home literacy practices was very evident. As Heath (1985) and Barton (1995) have both observed, children are steeped in a range of literacy practices before they start school, and much of what they regard as 'literacy' is their employment of literacy skills within a social setting. The shopping list was one example of this, as was the Sainsbury's bag inscribed by a child. This use of environmental print was re-enforced by the presence of cereal packets and cast-off boxes, on which the children would note the letters. Sometimes special letters, such as the letters of the child's name, were cut out and used in another context. Children were able to 'read' the packets of cereal they especially liked. They could identify certain of the promotions on packets, and often asked me to help them cut out particular characters featured on them. Environmental print was a useful starting point for a number of discussions and topics in the nursery: as well as 'shopping', the children discussed food, transport, road safety and health issues, using information they had 'read' around them.

Modelling and making things also stimulated talk, which could later become writing. For example, one morning two children made a model of a car wash using card on a base of card. They had obviously found the experience significant and the models provided an ideal opening to discuss car washes and then use the computer to generate writing. Many of the models the children made were triggers for discussions.

There was ample evidence to support Vygotsky's idea of writing as being supported by a 'sea of talk'. As the children created, they set up new meanings within the nursery. New stories were articulated and could be told. This process has particular implications for teachers of children from diverse social and cultural backgrounds. Too many storybooks and pictures commonly available in nursery schools do not represent the experience of the children. Nursery teachers need to be sensitive to the stories and meanings that children bring to the nursery. Model making seemed to provide an opportunity for children to make 'their' world real. Free model making, in three dimensions, allows children to 'realise' their worlds fully and bring into the nursery new thoughts and ideas. The actual process of making can develop narrative within children's minds. Often model making unlocked new areas not suggested by the nursery staff. The third dimension offered a sense of realism to the children, which they exploited to the full.

Model making was also a response to narrative. Many models were a direct reflection of books the children enjoyed – the effect upon the children of *The Tiny Seed* has been mentioned. Many children employed narratives from videos and television programmes they enjoyed, such as

Figure 4.7

101 Dalmations, or Batman and Spiderman. *Peter Pan* and *The Ugly Duckling* were other subjects of model making. Narrative often structured the children's models, as the story developed while they were making them.

The children were also investigating the grammar of visual design as they worked. Many models were made according to how they wanted a thing to look, and the design element came to the fore. A particular shape, such as the insides of toilet rolls, would suggest an item to the child, as when two such items together made a pair of binoculars. In this instance, it was the shape of the object that created an idea in the children's minds. Sometimes narrative and form worked together as an object was being made. For example, Abigail's fish probably has its origins in both the *Rainbow Fish* story and her father's computer screen saver, but she was also interested in how the object looked. Here narrative and design were working together.

Another form of literacy encouragement was the children's kinaesthetic appreciation of the alphabet and names. The teachers used three dimensions to encourage the children to experience letters. They were often reminded of letter shapes as they worked – one child, on her way to making a car wash model, remarked 'that's a letter A, it's in my name' as she cut out an A type shape.

In the picture opposite, children have represented the letter 'S' as a series of snakes (See Figure 4.7). The snakes curl down from the letters, giving them a three dimensional aspect and providing a concrete image for the children to take hold of the letter 'S'. Putting these Ss across the classroom like a washing line gave them a new sense of reality – hanging in space. Such forms established the 'reality' of the alphabet to the children. 'Cutting out' letters was a favoured occupation in the nursery.

Likewise, children used sand and glue to make raised models of the first letter of their names. The links between their names and, for example, their bodies or handprints was often emphasised in discussion about the form and shape of the letters. The body was a learning tool, their fingers used to count, represent letters and squidge letters from playdough or make biscuits of letter shapes. Often children made jigsaws using letters, or cut out letters to make a pattern. Letters and the body were joined as a physical experience. Rounded fingers made an 'o' shape, and many children used their fingers to spell out the first letter of their names.

Implications for practice in nursery classrooms

- **Making things more real**

  Modelling provides young children with an opportunity to make their experience real. As Kress points out, once an object is 'cut out' it acquires a new realism and becomes animated. Free modelling in particular is an opportunity for children to represent their world.

- **Bodies and space**

  Children's relationship with their bodies is profound. Using large cardboard boxes and small baskets in the nursery allowed them a way of describing their bodily relationship with the outside world. Activities such as mask making can channel that interest.

- **Becoming larger**

  The making of things can provide meaning for children in terms of what is happening to them. Many models produced by the children had deep significance. Mask making and dressing up gave them scope to express powerful emotions. Being 'powerless' small children could be remedied by dressing up in high heels or as 'Superman'.

- **Hearing the story**

  Narrative and telling stories can be expressed through model making. It is important to recognise influence from books, classroom activities, media, videos, home, cultural background or other children. For example, Zainab's penguin was almost certainly a result of my reading her a book about penguins.

- **Symbolic structures**

  What the children make can generally be described as symbolic. Any activity in which children are trying to describe complex thoughts such as: where do I come from? by using symbol is highly significant – take, for instance, the account of seeds and shopping discussed in the last chapter. Teachers need to recognise that they are dealing with profound thoughts and emotions which transcend the external content. The use of symbol in model making can be extended to activities that come later, such as creative writing and poetry.

- **Supporting design and technology interests**

  Children are exploring their interest in the design of the material – whether in the shapes, material or form. Many were interested in the texture of the material they worked with. It is important to credit at this stage the design implications of what the children are doing. Many children were interested in making shapes; it was part of a process of finding out how shapes worked and it stimulated discussions about shape (circles, squares and diamonds).

The third dimension offers children opportunities to explore, in a more tactile form, issues of space, material, form and design. They use different influences to create new structures, and often take the structural forms as a point of departure for new designs. They need opportunities to consider the structural and design elements of a model as well as its content.

Working with children requires attention to the focus they bring to the work they are engaged in, and a developed understanding of the influences, motivations and intentions of children making meaning in a variety of forms, even though it is sometimes difficult to work out what children are making. For example, in the case of Zainab's mosque, I had to wait until she finished before I was given the opportunity to find out what it was.

Working in the third dimension releases children to 'animate' their objects fully, as Kress indicates in his analysis of 'cutting out'. And it offers new symbolic opportunities. The heightened realism of objects presented in the three dimensions is very meaningful to young children. Nursery spaces must foster free modelling by children, as both a bridge to literacy and a form of narrative and design expression.

Chapter 5

Seeing is believing
Writing their names

Observation 4/10/96

I arrived to find no activities set up, so the teacher suggested I sit at a table and work with the children on tracing their names. Mutahhara, Becky, Barney and Abdul came and did some tracing over their names, and then some drawing. One tracing card was of a pattern. The children drew the pattern, then cut it out. Abigail wanted to make this into a bracelet and then so did Barney and Lydia. The children got scissors to cut up strips of paper or tracing paper and sellotape to make them into bracelets.

Literacy means different things to different people. To adults, it is the key to a huge range of possibilities. The skills of writing and reading help us to function effectively in everyday life. Literacy is highly valued in our culture, as initiatives such as the National Literacy Strategy and the National Year of Reading affirm. From this adult perspective, literacy is one of the hidden givens for a children entering school – they have entered school so as to learn to read and write.

To children themselves the position is different. Already, we assume, they have learned to talk and walk and play and eat a variety of foods. What concerns children who enter nursery are different issues. They are away from their parents; faced with unfamiliar children. Toys are available and also books, paints, construction toys and computers. To the children each activity is of equal importance. They see the added marks on the wall and beside their name pegs. They might already recognise these as script and identify their own names.

Writing can mean a number of things to children. It might mean the things that happen when you order a meal, or when your mother writes a shopping list. It may mean a first encounter with a letter. It may mean praise and encouragement, or frustration. At a closer level, writing involves pens, paper, and now the keyboard. Writing is making marks, of a squiggly nature. These marks have power. They mean self, and they mean the world. Writing is interpreted differently by different children.

The concepts of a child just starting to write can sometimes be startlingly different from those of the more experienced writer. To the beginner, writing may be an activity with rather less significance than drawing. Writing might even **be** drawing, as the child 'draws' a story, or 'writes' a page of looped lines. Children who are starting to write are engaging with what adults present to them as writing. Adults and children see the same task differently. For adults, writing requires an understanding of certain forms, such as loops. Children may see a loop as a face or an interesting curve. Their response to the task is to examine its form.

Children's relationship to writing, especially to the written form of their own name, is bound to be imbued with a particular meaning. The power of their name may transform a page or extend it into something different. Paying attention to how children see the kinaesthetic act of writing and the looped curves of the adult script reveals the complexity of the perceptual processes inside children's minds. This chapter seeks to examine the writing process through observation of the nursery children's work. It explores the connections between writing and drawing, and examines the process of learning to write one's own name. It also identifies how children perceive a given task. Observation of bracelet making revealed how a writing exercise can become employed in quite another creative activity by children who are 'reading' a given drawing in a particular way.

Drawing, play and writing

When children begin to make marks on a page, these generally take the shape of rounded circles. This initial scribbling might be motivated initially by simple interest in the effect of pen on paper – the experience of drawing as purely kinaesthetic. As children develop relationships with the signs on the page and the outside world, this scribbling becomes steadily more complex. The following example demonstrates this process (See Figure 5.1).

A three and a half year old has drawn the first initial of his name – B. Inside this B he has drawn little faces. When drawing the Bs he said:

Figure 5.1

'these are the babies'. The letter 'B' is linked in his mind to the alliterative word 'baby'. Even deeper is the link between the child at three and a half and the child as a baby. The large 'grown-up' B encloses the small babies. In one sense the 'B' is a symbol – it 'stands for' a baby. The form 'B' lends itself to the drawing of a shape because of its rounded structure. It can be used to express a form, like a head or a body. The child has 'animated' the letter B and produced little faces inside the letter to create small shapes with large heads and small bodies. The rounded shape has created the suggestion of a face.

This early symbolising and animating of alphabetic script gives us a clue to why literacy is, for children, so connected to form and how it cements the link between writing and drawing. The child has drawn a 'B' and drawn a baby inside it. Large eyes and a rounded shape suggest the wide eyes of a baby, but it is also clear that this is work on the alphabet; some of the shapes are As and some are Ps. The child is animating the alphabet. This can also be observed when illustrators make people out of the letters of the alphabet or animate the shapes to suggest such things as zoo animals or plants and flowers.

This example shows us how close drawing and writing are to children when they begin nursery school. Specialists in the early years have commented on the close links between writing, drawing, play and symbolising. Whitehead (1990), Dyson (1993), Barrs (1988) and Kress (1997), among others, have written about the links and overlaps between drawing and writing, and the connection with other activities such as play.

Drawing and writing accompanies play and is often part of a play structure. As Anne Haas Dyson observes:

> Young children's social lives are enacted primarily through symbolic media... initially print may simply be an interesting object to investigate or a useful prop for dramatic play (1993 p.79).

This idea of print as a 'prop' for dramatic play can be observed in action when, for example, children 'play' at restaurants and scribble down orders from pretend customers.

Print is symbolic; it is used to 'stand for' other things. The main function of print, as Vygotsky (1978, p. 28) observes, is to communicate. Many writers have commented on how children switch from drawing to writing and back again to make their communication clear. Barrs (1988) argues that for many children drawing continues to be an important element in writing, a means for symbolising meaning. Barrs' model, drawn from Vygotsky, is especially helpful in indicating the importance of symbolism in children's writing and drawing. Barrs also makes links between drawing, writing and narrative play. Children 'playing' restaurants might write down pictographic script using drawings to suggest certain items. The play, waiting at table, and the writing and drawing are woven together in the children's minds. Many nurseries make use of this enthusiasm for 'making marks' in the 'shop' or 'restaurant' set up in one part of the space. The exploring of script comes out of the child's awareness of how script fits into the adult world. I draw on this model of linked writing, drawing and dramatising in my observation of the children described in this chapter.

We look at two children who are in the process of writing their names. They were observed over a period of time – one child, my own, over two years. The contrasting observations show clearly how drawing and writing are initially intertwined and then move apart. And observing how children perceived a tracing exercise reveals the children's own perception of the task. Writing is intimately connected to form and generally form mirrors meaning. When examining children's writing or drawing one must understand the process by which the drawing is 'telling a story' or, equally important, is exploring form on a page. The process of observing children at work can reveal their motivation as well as unravel the processes by which an object comes to be made.

How writing was taught in the nursery
The children in the nursery were encouraged to learn to write their names. They wrote them on their drawings, where they produced very different spatial accounts of them.

As one way of teaching them to write, the teacher gave children tracing paper to follow the lines of their names, which he had written in lower case letters. These were displayed and the children were invited to copy their names on a sheet headed 'my name is'. This was underscored by ruled lines, allowing the children to write their names out several times. As a kinaesthetic exercise to appreciate the shape of each child's initial letter, they all made the letter that began their name out of sand and glue.

The sequence I observed in the nursery went thus:

1. First letter of name made with glue and sand

2. 'My name is' on tracing paper

3. 'My name is' on paper

4. Children encouraged to write their name on their work.

At the same time, the teachers had a number of different activities operating in the nursery. There were wooden letters for children to form their names; computer generated texts that the children could use to write their names on the keyboard; modelling clay to model letters; and they made letter shapes with pastry and paint and with blocks. The teachers allowed the children to use 'special pens' to write the letters of their names and encouraged them to think of literacy as a special activity by letting them use gold pens or attractive letters with which to form their names. Children were encouraged to feel and hold their initial letters and to look around them for evidence of print. Print and letters were given prominence and status within an environment that also valued drawing and modelling, so the children naturally integrated writing into their other activites. Thus making a picture with V-shaped strips of card suggested to one child the beginning of her name (an A) and also the shapes she wanted to create. She was working in both the realm of the alphabet and the realm of pure design. Often the V shape would float between being her initial letter and being a shape. Literacy was part of the wider picture of modelling and drawing, not separate but connected to other activities.

Children writing in the nursery

Observations revealed that the children often interpreted writing activities as drawing activities. They were interested in the task and were not made to feel that there was a formal content. Accordingly, tracing letters produced some interesting variations on the expected. One morning, I arrived to find no activities set up, so the teacher suggested I sit at a table and work with the children on 'tracing names'.

Mutahhara, Becky, Barney and Abdul came and did some tracing over their names, followed by some drawing. The children had been given a looped object to trace, similar to a chain since it was continuous and had loops on it. So the children 'read' it as the first step to making a bracelet. They started cutting out immediately after tracing, sticking the bracelet in place with sellotape. The resulting objects were chains of decorative circles, linked with sellotape, that the children wore proudly to go home (See figure 5.2).

Some children made rings and a butterfly. There was no hint from the teacher that this exercise had been misinterpreted. To the children, the natural response to the curved exercise was to make bracelets. They had no idea that this was an exercise to encourage joined up writing. Here is clear evidence of children reading the elements correctly in terms of their

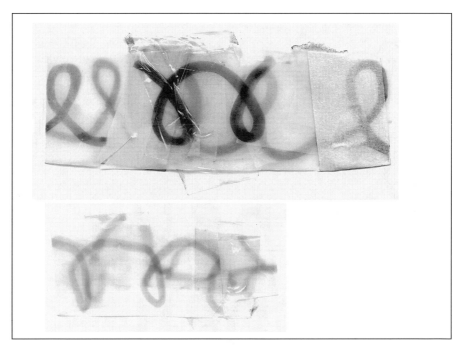

Figure 5.2

design potential. They see the exercise in terms of the shape and form of the figure they are given to copy. Their information is that this is a bracelet shaped object – so they read it as 'bracelet'. The concept of joined-up writing and tracing curves is not one with which they are familiar so they interpret the object's shape and form in the most plausible way.

Writing, too, can be differently interpreted. Sometimes when teachers slightly mis-represented a piece of script, the children, not knowing that this was a 'mistake', reproduced what they saw. For nursery children encountering script and print, seeing really is believing.

This was apparent when an adult wrote one child's name in black and then put dots on the second version for the child to copy. The child copied these faithfully, including the adult's mis-placing of the dots on the 'a'. He saw a little cross-line, and that the dots went across the shape of the 'a' and that is what he copied. Writing has become a process of copying a shape. The child is 'reading' the teacher's version of his own name (See Figure 5.3).

Below the traced name he has written his own account of his name at that time, done in capitals. Like many of the nursery children, he had been taught to use capital letters at home, so he 'reads' this version of his

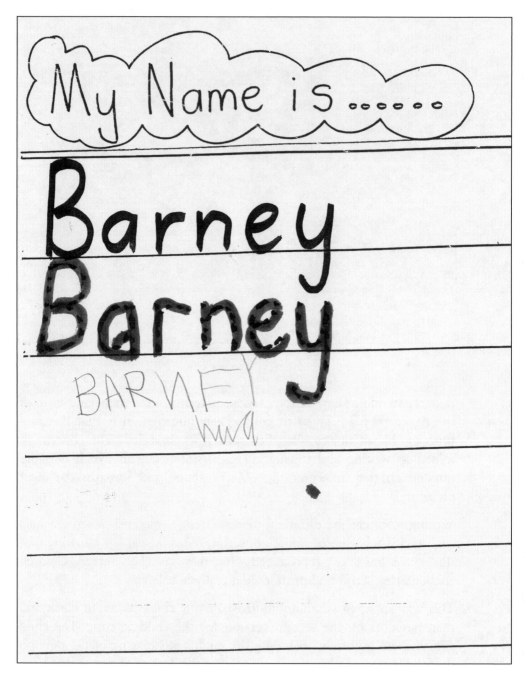

Figure 5.3

name in capitals. He has an internal picture of what his name is. He sees 'Barney' and then reproduces the essence of the name, as he as learnt to write it: BARNEY. This is an entirely accurate representation of his name, in his terms. To him this is not a copying exercise, but an exercise in writing his name.

To the child, these two tasks are crucially different. One involved copying – tracing over the adult's dots – which he read as a design exercise. The other, the reproduction of the name, involved his calling up his own inner version of his name. This exercise required subjective decisions about what constituted his name.

The next picture shows how he copied out his name, and then continued with his own versions of it. What is interesting about this example is that Barney assumed that the dots after 'my name is' are an important part of writing the name and so he reproduced the dots after he wrote his name. Again, the adult has not understood that, to the child, the dots are a significant piece of the writing. As children are interpreting and reading everything they see, they comprehend the dots as being part of the exercise. Inevitably, then, they will reproduce them (See Figure 5.4).

Children interpret the tasks they are given according to the information they have. They infuse activities with meanings which come from a complex mesh of thoughts and ideas. Sometimes, writing activities are a way of making symbols. The writing 'stands for' something else. To children the writing might be a drawing of something, whereas to the adult it resembles writing. Drawing and writing are both symbolising activities; ways in which children express their world. Their names are intensely symbolic to children; they represent them, and can 'stand for' them.

In some cases, the children's names and their drawings may be intertwined. The drawing by Mutahhara shows how she has used the same design process for both her name and her drawing of her family (see Figure 5.5).

In both the drawing and the writing, the 'legs' are long and spindly. Mutahhara sees her name as connected to her family. She 'draws' her name with the same design principles as she draws her family. Self and family-self, defined by their name, are intertwined.

This could be seen in the relationship children had with their name pegs. The process of writing their names is closely connected to children's sense of self. By writing their names, they are re-producing themselves. The characters have a meaning beyond that of an alphabetic structure.

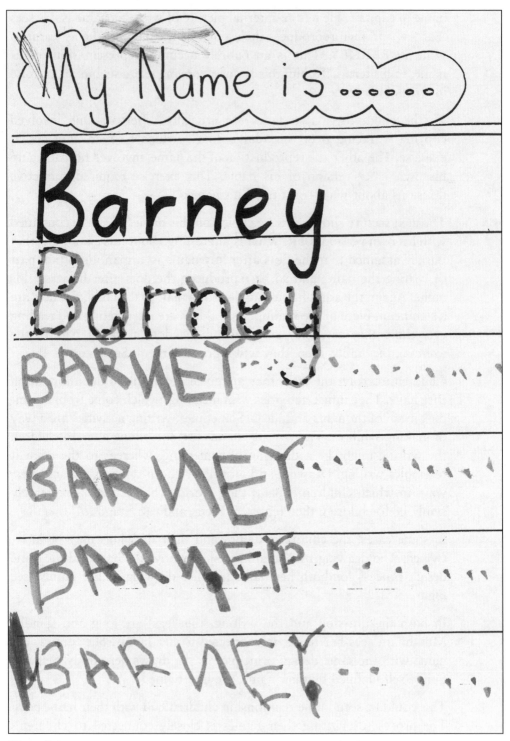

Figure 5.4

Figure 5.5

Learning to write

Following a child through the writing process reveals this clearly. In contrast to the earlier example of his page of Bs, we can see Barney developing a pattern for the letters of his name in Figure 5.6.

The letters are arranged in response to the space available on the page. The page has dictated the form of the letters. They are elongated to fill the page because Barney is responding to drawing on a page. His key motivation is to fill the page, and his purpose in drawing the letters is to display the knowledge of the page. The child has responded to the idea that to write is to fill a page with letters. Here, I would argue, the crucial motive is the form of the text, whereas the B-babies are motivated by symbolic reasons – 'here is my B and I am the baby'.

In the next example, the pattern has detached itself from the letters. There is an experience of lines on the page, this time quite deliberately enclosed (See Figure 5.7).

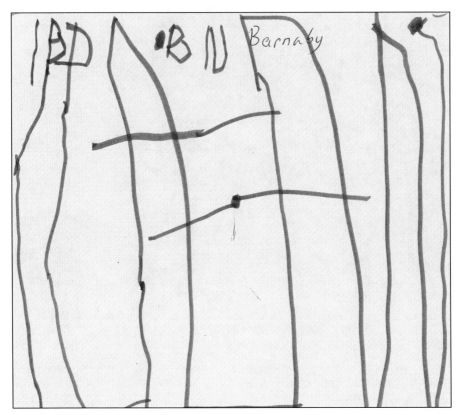

Figure 5.6

The letters are still not accurate but they are representations of some of the letters of Barney's name. The letters and the design on the page have become two separate things. The design mirrors the letters but is not part of them. It echoes the earlier form of criss-cross lines filling the page, but here it is enclosed. Barney has discovered the 'separateness' of writing. His illustration is a reflection of the writing of the letters but it is separate.

I observed Mutahhara following a similar process. In Mutahhara's writing, Figure 5.5 shows how closely the drawing and the script are intertwined, with the length of the legs of the people reflecting the length of the letters of her name. She wrote it when she was three and three quarters. The name is misspelled, but this is partly because she is responding to the writing and drawing task in terms of its design rather than a need for accuracy. Both letters and legs are part of a wider conception, to do with the length of a line and its relation to a body. Mutahhara is connecting the writing with the drawing. She is drawing her name and her family as part of a wider whole. She is, as Mutahhara, inextricably bound up with her family. She draws them in the same style

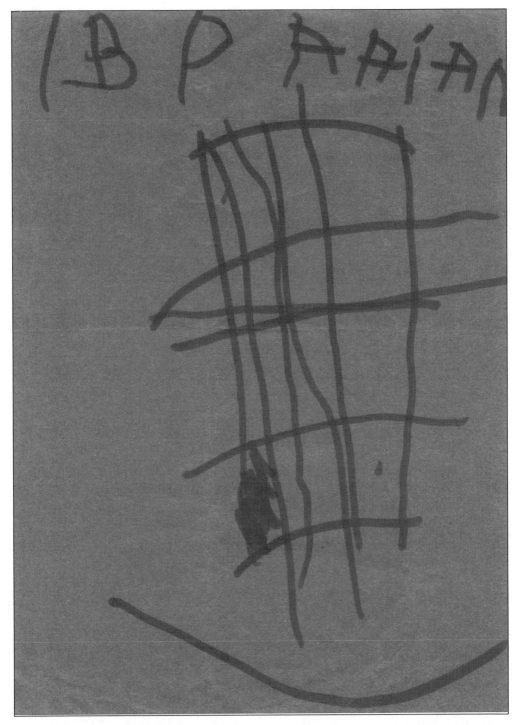

Figure 5.7

Figure 5.8

as she draws her name, with long legs and small bodies. The connection between writing and drawing is very close. Mutahhara's later versions of her name reveal a gradual progression to lower case script, and to a pre-occupation with her name at the expense of the drawing. In Fig 5:8 she has used the masking tape to emphasise her name, and the formless squiggle shows that she is less focused on the drawing. The 4, again emphasised with tape, is given significance – she has recently turned four. Mutahhara has discovered the primacy of script in her world (See Figure 5.8).

How children perceive the task of writing is immensely complex. Writing and drawing are symbolic activities. Children make marks on the paper for a reason. As they become interested in the page, the focus shifts to a connection with the page and engagement with its form. These two processes may happen at the same time. At this stage, their response is to the page, and writing becomes a task connected to page layout. The development is to do with the ordering of letters, beginning with a representation of some of the letters, as shown in the work of both Barney and

Mutahhara, and culminating in a capitalised version of their names. In Barney's case this version persisted in spite of the teacher's attempts to teach him lower case script.

Children are looking carefully at the form of the object in order to understand what it means, as we saw with Barney's attempt to read 'a'. The bracelet making exercise reveals the inventiveness of these children as they use what they have been given to interpret and transform their world. This demonstrates the complexity of the process of learning to write. With his capital letters, Barney produced a version of his name that is his own internal version. He has 'read' the word 'Barney' but has come up with his own version of his name. His reading uncovers the process of making an **'internal sign'** (Kress 1997 p.58). The child sees an object, internalises the sign, and then develops his own reading of this object – which is then reproduced. By uncovering the stages of learning to write, we can observe children's sign making in action. Cultural experience informs this process, as do the perceptions by children of what is there. Their interpretations may be regarded by adults as a 'misreading' of the task. In fact, the adult provided the elements and these were read correctly by the child – in terms of what they saw. The wider meaning of writing, and particularly joined up writing (as in the tracing exercise) are not apparent to the child.

What we are observing here is the point at which the children's identity is bound up with what they are producing. Mutahhara's work shows this transition from the initial intertwining of the writing, drawing and her self-portrait, to a deliberate separation of script and drawing. By tracking this process, we can uncover different stages through which the children went and illuminate how print finally becomes externalised.

Using symbols and animation to re-produce a concept is another form of externalisation – the page of Bs animated by Barney to form little babies is an example. This animating process can be linked to the interest children later take in 'cutting out' – a further stage in animation. The three-dimensional letters emphasised their 'realness' to the children in the nursery. They had experienced print in a variety of mediums: as letters in sand, as cut-out strips of card, as marks on a piece of paper, as parts of the body curled into letters. By feeling their way into print, the children could enjoy the letters for what they were – interesting shapes which sometimes connected to their selves, a connection formed through the first letter, or all the letters of their name. Also important was the form. Children recognised their names in terms of its overall form, and used the pattern in their accompanying drawings. Many children used alphabetic shapes in modelling, to enhance stories or develop a narrative. For example, the large A was often chosen by children whose name began with an A, to describe something they had done. Print's relationship with story and information was mediated by the children's response to these curved shapes and interesting patterns.

Literacy in action – improving practice

Children can be encouraged to use print creatively by adopting a wider and more fluid engagement with literacy activities, as indicated by the observation findings outlined in this chapter:

- **Writing and the self**
  It is possible to see early literacy activities as a starting point for discussions about the children's sense of self and their experiences. In turn, children may be encouraged to 'draw a story' and use their narratives to write in 'pretend writing'. The story can be enlivened by print. Children's drawings are scattered with small pieces of print, which takes the drawing into a different dimension. Print may signify a number of things for a child: adult status, a particular shape, or a circle in which to hide.

- **Play and writing**
  That children can 'play' with writing needs to be recognised. Rather than compelling children to do writing as we recognise it, it is more fruitful to let children value their writing as a form of representation equal to other vital forms of communication. Children's sense of space, the arc of their arms and the curve of a round shape on the page, are all forms of representation. To identify and over-emphasise one element may keep children away from all other forms. Exploring shape, the space on a page and the feel of a sheet of paper, are just as important.

- **Use of capital letters**
  Upper and lower case letters are often interpreted differently by children. Barney, for instance 'read' the teacher's lower case letters as being his name, but nonetheless wrote it 'his way' – in capitals. He visualises his name written in one way while the teacher sees it in another. To force him to change would undermine his developing sense of competence. Again, it is the child's interpretation of the lines on the page that needs to be understood.

The points above can be situated in the wider context of learning to write. The SCAA *Desirable Outcomes on Entry to Compulsory School-*

ing illustrate how literacy activities in the nursery relate to the National Curriculum in England:

Of children's attainment on entry to school the government asks that:

> In their writing they use pictures, symbols, familiar words and letters to communicate meaning, showing awareness of some of the different purposes of writing. They write their names with appropriate use of upper and lower case letters (SCAA, 1996).

Seeing the awareness of writing as part of a wider developmental framework that includes pictures and symbols, fits in with my analysis. Children's writing can be understood as a complex mesh of symbol making and beginning writing, in which they link words, pictures and symbols.

The Language and Literacy section of the SCAA *Desirable Outcomes* states that children should 'recognise letters of the alphabet by shape and sound'. My observations show that children are going much further than this in their work with the alphabet and with the shapes they need to learn to write. They are combining the alphabet with an understanding of shape and body and mass. They are thinking laterally, and using a wider dimensional structure to understand what is expected of them. Thus their frame of reference is actually wider than the fairly narrow requirements of SCAA.

The most important issue is how children see their names. The initial letter may 'stand for' the child in a number of complex ways, and may even be a picture of them. Once the children's teachers or parents comprehend this, they can see how children relate to text. Stories and ideas can flow from children's production of written text in an inventive and exciting way. From the beginnings of making marks on a page come children's relation to the world and to their selves. Before they learn to write they undergo a process as demanding, complex and exciting as the activity itself. In our hurry to encourage children to write we tend to forget to value the creative activities of children before they start writing. These inventive constructions of mark and squiggle may mean as much as the faithfully copied text. If we pay attention to the marks children make, their interest can be extended and their delight in drawing acknowledged. Writing for children means many things, and all of them can be celebrated.

Chapter 6

Try to see it my way
Making a princess

Observation (5/11/96)

Barney began to draw his usual princesses. He did about six, and asked me to help him do the T-shirt. Abigail drew her princess, and then began to cut it out. She said she was going to make an envelope to put the princess in. Other children came up and did some drawing for a while. Joe drew a robot, and William came and hovered around. Abdul stayed at the table but did no drawing. Abigail continued with her princess. She began to focus on providing the princess with clothes, which she cut out and stuck on. The princess became 3D. Abigail got me to help her make the envelope. She decided it was a bag, and put a clasp on it, then began to decorate the bag elaborately.

This chapter looks closely at the work of children in the nursery in terms of the cultural experiences they bring to their model making. By observing children at work, we can uncover their cultural and geographical internal images. Understanding how children internalise the images they receive helps us realise how children take in and then develop the images around them, and our ideas about how children make meaning in a shared 'imaginative universe' (Geertz, 1973 p.13) will be extended. This chapter explores the concept of shared social meanings.

It is morning, and the children are sitting at the modelling table, putting strips of card onto pieces of paper. I am watching, but cannot tell what is being made. On the walls of the nursery, all around the children, I can see images: of 'my body'; 'the park'; instructions; writing; computers; pieces of everyday life described and displayed for the children to see and learn from. The children continue to model. One little girl is busy putting a variety of coloured strips onto her piece of card. We wait to see what it is. Within the repertoire of images she habitually carries in her mind are a number of possibilities – perhaps the house of the first little pig, perhaps a picture of 'my house'. She finishes and turns to me proudly.

She has covered the piece of paper with thin strips of paper, and put a complex pattern of overlaying paper on it. There is an object submerged beneath it. 'What is it?' I ask. 'It's a car wash, of course', says the child. The pieces of paper are the brushes that cover the car. Her main efforts have been directed to covering over the car thickly. This child has set out to represent in the nursery her experience of going to the car wash and has chosen a theme that lies outside my expectations. The collage forms a sign, which is socially constructed and which stands for 'car wash'. The child has 'read' the situation of being inside a car, has transformed the experience inside her head and has then reproduced it as 'car wash'.

When children create something, be it a piece of writing, a drawing or a model, the making of the object is infused with their experience of the world. It is crucial for adults working with young children in the nursery to grasp this, because the experience of the teacher and helpers will not always be the same as the experience of the children. We carry around visual images in our minds and these are attached to certain concepts. While the idea of a 'crown' is accessible to some readers, others will be more familiar with the image of a *chador*. When we think of religion, the image that may spring to mind may be of a sickle-shaped moon at the top of a mosque, a cross on a church spire or an entirely different symbol. When we notice something, we check our observation against what we have experienced before. When we are asked to provide an image, we provide it from the stock of images we habitually carry.

While nursery teachers are aware of the importance of valuing the culture of the children they work with, they may not share that culture. The teachers sometimes did not recognise certain of the children's creations for what they were, simply because they did not have a visual image of the model in their own minds.

I came into the nursery one morning to find the children were working with bits of silver card. These were shaped like this:

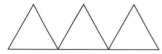

and like this

The connection was quickly established when Martha brought in a crown from home, and wanted to make a crown with the shapes. This idea took on, and soon Georgia, Becky and Martha were making and decorating their crowns. Zainab also became interested but I was surprised when she wanted to put the oval-shaped fabric round her head, so that it surrounded her face. Surprised, that is, until I remembered Fatima, her mother. Fatima wore a *chador*, and her face was framed by a piece of material, making an oval shape. Zainab was using as her reference point the *chador*, not a crown. The strips of silver card gave her an opportunity to represent a grown-up female in what was to her an accessible image – unlike a crown. She was interested in exploring what she looked like when she dressed up 'like her mummy' and naturally she would create a sign different from the one we were acculturated to expect. This little girl was exploring her definitions of femininity, and resisting our attempts to encourage her to turn into a western-style princess.

Princesses are extraordinarily important to these nursery children; they seem to ascribe strong emotions to the princess figure, and there are also clear connections with Disney. They often watch *The Swan Princess, Sleeping Beauty* and *Cinderella*. Few princesses are anything other than white and Western fairytale blue-eyed blondes, whereas the children in the nursery come from a variety of cultural backgrounds. Real life does nothing to counter these images. Diana was the real life princess most frequently mentioned, arousing strong emotions in the children – both before and after her death. The princess making described here was carried out while she was still alive, but she remains in the children's minds as the immediate image of 'princess'.

I watched a group of children draw and cut out princesses. They sat at the modelling table, on which was some red stiff paper and colouring pens. Abdul had begun to draw, using some new rainbow crayons. He said he was drawing a person. He cut out bits of paper and stuck them on, but he put them all over the figure, which took a long time. Most children were by now busy making princesses, which they then put into handbags.

Abdul had produced something entirely different. At the time I wondered why Abdul had totally covered up his princess. I couldn't see the point of making something so beautiful and then covering it over. What I failed to ask myself was: whose image of a princess were we dealing with? What were the internal images that the children connected to princesses, and what did I, as observer, miss in that initial observation?

First, there was Barney's princess. Barney had asked me to 'do the T-shirt' (see Observation Notes at the beginning of the chapter). Barney's internal image of a princess was of a woman who wears a T-shirt. I did not question this 'reading' of a princess – it coincides with my own internal image of a princess as a woman who wears T-shirts and attends a gym, just as the press was portraying Princess Diana at the time. Clearly, Barney and I shared the same internal image of a Princess. In the next version, done during the princess-making session, the princess has a star on her chest, and long hair and a long dress (see Figure 6.1).

This also fits with a Western ideal – the Cinderella princess with long hair. The star is possibly a jewel. Many of the children made crowns and stuck jewels on themselves as part of a general interest in royal wear. The children often referred to the images of Cinderella and Sleeping Beauty from the Disney films.

But Abdul's princess was different. I couldn't see why Abdul had resisted the usual pattern of princesses bedecked with jewels. His version is an elongated figure covered with pieces of cut up paper. It does reflect Abdul's interest in cutting and sticking. But this princess clearly was not wearing a T-shirt – she was almost completely covered (see Figure 6.2).

Abdul has covered the face of his princess with one piece of paper, and then placed more pieces over the entire body, which – beneath the covering – has been coloured in bright, attractive colours. The impression is of a person who is very attractive, brightly coloured and tall, with a small head, who is then concealed. I did not realise the significance of this until later.

While I was sitting at the dentist one day with my children, Abdul and his sisters came in. They were a lively, friendly group, but in this formal space, they all sat still, with their young brother, who gazed solemnly at me. All the sisters wore coverings over their hair. And when I met her in the playground, I saw that Abdul's mother was fully veiled. The family is from Somalia.

Abdul's representation of a princess was of a person who is brightly coloured and tall, covered by a robe. He had reproduced his version of a 'princess' to incorporate his own experience. Princess equals woman equals a person with colourful clothes beneath a *chador*. The process of transformation of the sign 'princess' incorporated his cultural experience. Abdul had retained this internal image of a princess even though the children around him produced very different representations. For now, he had retained his stock of internal images, notwithstanding

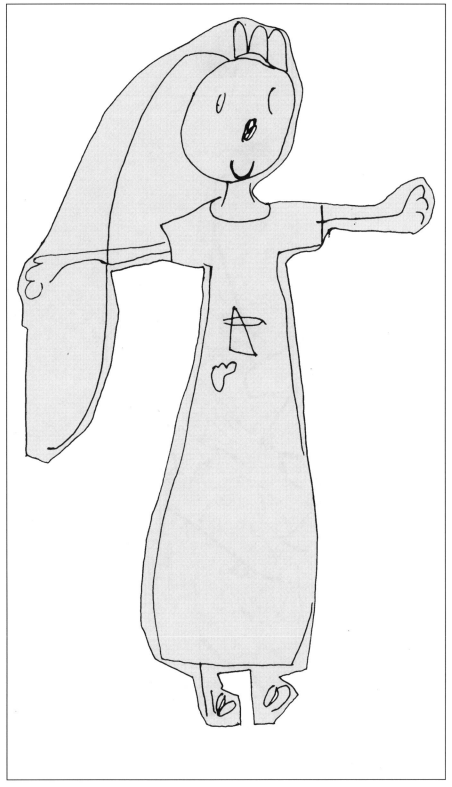

Figure 6.1

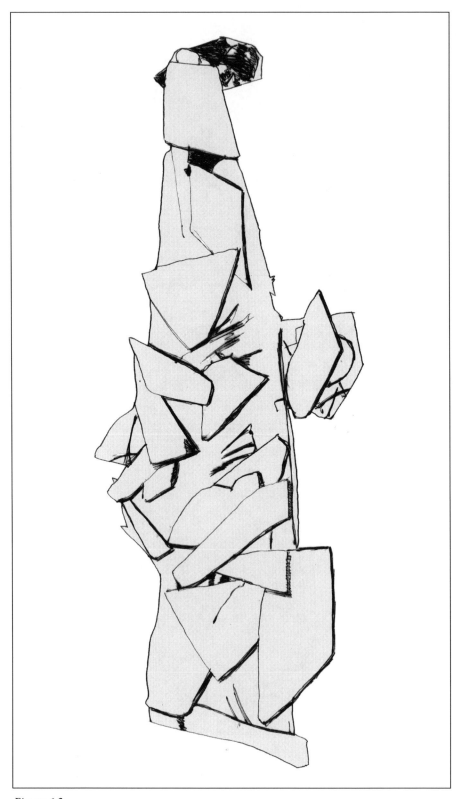

Figure 6.2

the prevailing images of princesses. Recognition of Abdul's princess was a vital part of recognition of Abdul, of his inner thoughts and life.

By contrast, Barney's reading of the concept 'Princess' gives her long hair (accentuated) and a long dress with a star on it. The figure smiles, and it has fingers and toes. Barney's reading of 'princess' comes closer to representations of his sister (who has long hair) or his reading of Disney films such as *Cinderella* and *Sleeping Beauty*. Here, princess equals woman equals his mother or sister, or Cinderella. Abdul's 'reading' of a princess is different. He has taken the concept of 'veiled woman' available to him, and reproduced this as his version of 'princess'. Here is a clear example of a child internalising an image and reproducing it, in spite of the other versions available on the table before him.

In a later observation, Mutahhara then four and one month drew herself. She is a small Bangladeshi child who generally wore a little frilly skirt, jumper and tights. She is never veiled and never wears long dresses. However, here she draws herself wearing a full-length *chador* (See Figure 6.3).

Again, the child is reproducing the image of herself in light of a wider cultural sign – the female person in her culture. In one sense, this is a bleak appraisal of the choices open to her as she grows up but in another sense, it is a positive affirmation of Mutahhara within her space. She can be this person within the nursery because the nursery accepts it, and recognition that her interpretation of herself as this person draped in a long dark gown is important in affirming her sense of self.

The children in the nursery with Islamic heritage were often working against the cultural expectations of their teachers. I later observed Zainab's mosque. Zainab had spent the morning making pictures using blue card. She was the child who had earlier made a car wash; now she cut out a strip of card and placed it at right angles to her picture, so that it soared into the sky. She placed some masking tape horizontally across the picture. She collected some black tissue paper, cut it out and stuck it to the bottom of the picture. On the other side of the paper she extended the masking tape a little way and tied it in a loop.

She began to talk: 'This is the door and here you go in, and here we sit, and here the boys sit...'. It took me a long time to understand what Zainab was saying. 'What is this?' I asked, pointing to the black stuff. 'This is where the boys sit', said Zainab patiently. I was wondering whether Zainab had made an aeroplane, a house or another car. I could see the point of the door knob but not of the strong line going across the

Figure 6.3

picture. 'And this is where we sit', said Zainab, pointing to the top right-hand corner of the picture. Light began to dawn. 'It is a mosque', said Zainab, stating what to her was obvious. Zainab had produced a sign which created the essence of the mosque. It was divided into a space for her and her mother, and another for her brothers and father. This was the essential fact of the mosque for her, and it was translated into a sign. A form of transformation had been achieved, as the small girl related her personal experience to the nursery world.

When I pointed this out to the teacher, he was astonished, and acknowledged that his own internal image bank, too, was culturally specific. We began to realise that the children's minds were capable of reproducing images new to the nursery. Zainab had reproduced a new image for us that was not available in the images on the wall or in the books she read. (Note: The mosque was taken home by Zainab's mother, who admired it. When I asked her for the picture, she said she was very sorry but it had got lost at home. Sadly, this was the fate of many of the children's drawings!)

The examples described here could be taken from any inner city nursery, and many teachers will have noticed this process for themselves. The theoretical background to the processes I was watching merits consideration here.

Vygotsky's concept of internalisation

The process of meaning making results from a dynamic interchange between stored concepts in a child's mind and the outside world. Vygotsky (1978, p.56) describes internalisation as: 'the internal reconstruction of an external operation'. In other words, the child reconstructs internally in response to an external event. He observes that: 'the process of internalisation consists of a series of transformations' and describes the process thus:

> Firstly the external activity being understood internally, secondly the interpersonal process is transformed into an intrapersonal one, and finally the transformation occurs as part of a long series of developmental events (Vygotsky, 1978, p.56-7).

Transformation is here understood as a process that takes place in a complex series of shifts in the mind. Vygotsky's theory of 'internalisation' points to the dynamic nature of the child's interpretative processes. In this theoretical structure, Zainab would go to a mosque, internally reconstruct the experience, and move into an external understanding of the event which is then transformed in her mind into an external event. This is the new sign she had produced – 'mosque'.

The internal sign

Another way of understanding this process is to characterise Zainab's mosque as an 'internal sign'. Here is her own reading of 'mosque' which she then reproduces as a new sign. According to Gunther Kress the process of creating a new sign involves the creation of an 'internal sign' (Kress, 1997 p.58).

The internal sign is made whenever children 'read' (in the widest sense) another sign – a drawing, story, or piece of text. The internal sign is culturally specific to the children's own experience. The children's internal sign-making is informed by their internal structures and ideas. The internal structure with which each child has grown up includes the cultural expectations they carry within them. When they reproduce the sign children are also reproducing their cultural environment.

Reading the world

When she made her mosque, Zainab was providing us with a new text. She had 'read' her world in her own way.

> Reading is a transformative action, in which the reader makes sense of the signs provided to her or to him within a frame of reference of their own experience, and guided by their interest at the point of reading (Kress 1997 p.58).

This idea of 'reading' as akin to 'interpreting' or 'taking in' in turn evokes a response: sign making. Even if that is an internal process, it is an important one to track. In this case, the internal sign making by Abdul, Mutahhara and Zainab differed from the internal signs made by Barney. While I, as observer, accepted Barney's princess with a T-shirt because I recognised the reference, the princess made for me by Abdul was one that I had to learn to recognise. Abdul had actively 'read' his world, produced his own sign, and used his internal transforming skills to create a specific reading of the term 'princess'. Likewise, Zainab was working counter to the images around her when she produced the new image 'mosque'.

Composing and culture

All this activity is shaped by culture. Children bring their stored culture to their composing and making activities and this in turn permeates what they do. The media, from turtles to Teletubbies, Princess Diana to Cinderella, influences this culture but most important is the children's experience of their families and their world. The child of a woman who wears a *chador* weaves this mother into stories and models. Much of the narrative interest in the model making came from experiences outside the classroom. Children made mosques, Spidermen or car wash images which were meaningful to them. Their social worlds sometimes interacted and sometimes they did not. Sometimes the teachers were able to identify the children's model, and sometimes the children had to explain what their model meant to them. While many models were generated by classroom activity, what went on outside shaped and dictated much of the work. This meant that a task was interpreted differently by different children.

To the children, culture was not tempered with the markers that adults place on it. The children regarded books and videos as equal sources of ideas, and did not value one over the other. They referred to *Peter Pan* as both a book and a video and had no idea which came first. Many children thought *Cinderella* was just a video and were unaware of a book version. The children swapped conversation about what they enjoyed. At the time of writing, Teletubbies had taken hold, so the children did have some shared culture. The observations also revealed however, that the children interpreted this culture very differently – only some were influenced by Disney, for instance. Tinkerbell was available as 'thing to be' for some boys but others thought that they could only be Superman or Batman.

The culture of the school affected the children in the selection of images that were made available. In the nursery where I observed, the pictures on the walls were of children's drawing, of a fire station, a description of healthy foods, the alphabet, and of women as engineers. There were no images from Disney or the Teletubbies. What would have happened if they were? What children produced was often 'at odds' with the classroom culture.

Children often create a complex assembly of different cultural experiences in one text. The Little Mermaid might have a hat belonging to Mary Poppins and the face of a Barbie doll. Children in the nursery used Disney characters, but moved them in and out of fantasy play, often transforming them as they did so. Different texts are mixed up to create new places where play can be explored. This mode of play is bound up with surfaces, and how things seem. But play arises essentially out of social context. Children play within meanings they recognise and construct new meanings from material they already use. Dyson (1993) describes this process as 'symbol weaving'. There is a mesh of different cultural influences with which children interact when they play, design, model or draw and this frees up their interpretation of these influences. As Dyson (1993, p.223) puts it:

> Childhood may well be a time when we more freely exploit the cultural material around us, having not yet fully discovered the fences society may erect between the 'high or proper' cultural stuff and the 'low'.

Children are boundary crossers – they move from one cultural space, such as the Spice Girls, to another, such as fairies. Children draw on the world of 'highly valued' culture and the world of 'popular' culture in more equal and impartial ways than adults do, and are able to construct meanings from both. This form of cultural weaving permeated the classroom I observed. Children grew into different roles according to which book or video they had recently seen. One little girl asked me to make her a Cruella de Vil cloak; another wanted a penguin suit. One child wanted a princess crown; another wanted to make a *chador*. Images from everyday life and fairytale, the natural world and Disney sat comfortably with each other. The children engaged actively with the media. Much of their model making expressed these influences. These models can be described as signs formed from a complex variety of such influences. Whitehead (1990) stresses the importance of linking home and school in order to create shared meanings, and of children's doing and making and their links forward to literacy:

> Sharing meanings is a richly complex feature of human behaviour and literacy will not be promoted by simply sticking to books and talk about books. The experiences children bring to school and the new experiences they find there must be re-enacted or tried out in many different symbolic ways – drawing and painting materials, dressing up clothes and play artefacts, moulding and sculpting media and construction equipment and natural objects. These are the foundations of early literacy and not 'optional extras' that might bridge the gap between home and school or help children settle in early. It is not the actual things that bridge the home-school gap and make for emotional security, it is what children are doing with and through them that enables the children to feel 'at home' in the world and culture of school and make their own significant contributions to it (Whitehead, 1990 p.177).

Shared social worlds enhance meaning, asserts Dyson (1993). When the children I observed made princesses, each made a different version. The images made by those who inhabited the same social world were understood more quickly by the adults, both of them – teacher and researcher – from the dominant cultural group.

Dyson (1993) argues that it is crucial to value the children's social worlds and to see composing activities as shaped by those worlds. The idea of language and signs as being socially constructed and shaped is important in explaining why different children produce different representations of the world. Drawn shapes change according to who is drawing them and according to the motivation and experience of the creator.

The examples discussed here demonstrate how important the social and cultural influences are on the minds of children. While Barney's princess has affinities with both the Disney *Cinderella* and Princess Diana, Abdul and Zainab present us with images which come from different cultural experiences. The word 'princess' has been filtered through the minds of Abdul and Barney to produce quite different accounts. The process of internalisation followed by external realisation has been caught in this observation.

Improving practice in nursery schools

- **The classroom walls**
  When they select images to display on the walls, teachers need to think about the limits of how they see the world. It could be that the children have entirely different ideas of what is important to them. Pictures of car washes and mosques may be more meaningful to urban children in an inner city area than pictures of farms and green fields.

- **Letting in new meanings**
  Parents and teachers can acknowledge different worlds and different perceptions of the world. Sometimes our interpretation of what a child produces is developed from the stock of images inside our heads. So we will see alphabetic meaning in the letter A, although this could, equally, be read as a structural shape unconnected to the alphabet. Seeing things from the child's perspective allows us to let in new meanings and new ideas.

- **Group processes**
  Children can be encouraged to work together, and to share particular meanings. Although Power Rangers may be of great interest to the boys in the class, teachers could extend the concept to include the interests of the other children. The theme of Transformation could be extended to include the major transformations related in myths and fairy stories, including a wide variety of sources and roles for children to engage in, such as the Ugly Duckling, Cinderella and so on.

- **Supporting shared narratives**
  Narrative can be used to bind the children's work together, either by encouraging the play activities of children into modelling, or by developing narratives in a shared structure. For example, a story such as the *The Very Hungry Caterpillar* can become a focus for a wide variety of activities, such as trying out new foods.

- **Parental involvement**
  To create a flow of influence from home to school, parental participation should be encouraged whenever possible. Following discussions with parents, it should be possible to represent the home life of all the children at the nursery.

This chapter emphasises the importance of attending to what children know – what Geertz (1993) calls the 'local knowledge' they carry within them. Every neighbourhood has its specific characteristics, landmarks, cultural symbols and messages. The children living there observe these landmarks. Car washes and mosques may form part of one neighbour-hood, another might feature sheep and cows. Both are valid, but which is more visible in the school nursery? By listening to children and by understanding their modelling, we can recognise the neighbourhoods they inhabit. And the internal bank of cultural images carried within each child can be similarly acknowledged and brought to life. The world of the nursery can and should reflect the outer, local world of the street, the park and the car wash.

Chapter 7

'The Power Ranger is fighting the baddies'
Boys and meaning making

Observation 12/11/96

I came in to find a lot of noise – it was raining. Some children were fighting in the home corner. 'We are cowboys,' said Andre. He had a basket on his head, which he said was a gladiator's helmet. He had worn it most of the morning. Some of the boys had strips of masking tape and bits of cardboard on them. This related to a game they had played this morning – 'We ran out of masking tape,' said the teacher.

Observation 20/9/96

Andre cut and glued some wings so that he could be Tinkerbell. He was very pleased with this. Some of the children's drawings had been put up, uncluding one of a Power Ranger having a fight.

Observation 5/11/96

We started by talking about Power Rangers. Jack did me a Power Ranger, and Lucy drew a car. Jack began a second Power Ranger.

Parents of boys in reception classes tend to be anxious nowadays. Ahead loom Standard Assessment Tests (SATS) which consistently show boys to be underperforming in reading and writing. In Year One, at aged six to seven years, the majority of the children attending reading recovery were boys. On entry to school in LEAs doing baseline testing, girls tested higher overall than boys in pre-literacy skills. Girls tend to do better at activities such as tracing letters, sounding out words and fine motor skills and comprehension – important skills for preparation for reading and writing. Girls are perceived as being more obedient and less troublesome than boys in the early years. Boys tend to 'run around' and be 'unconstructive', and are less likely than girls to be 'on task'.

However, when parents or teachers are asked about what boys in reception classes actually do, back come the replies:

'He builds models all day'; 'He is fine if he is building lego'; 'He plays with his cars in the sand all day long'. The parent who made the last statement added, 'But he must have been doing something right, because in the following year he read straight away'.

The boys in the research project I undertook were observed doing the following:

fighting
playing
drawing
making models
doing collage
sitting and looking at books
working on the computer
sorting beads
using bikes and outdoor equipment
listening, talking and writing.

Among the subjects that engaged them and that they used in play and modelling included:

Power Rangers
Batman
Spiderman
Captain Hook
Tinkerbell
The Ugly Duckling
Trucks, cars, ships, tanks, trains, boats and binoculars
Princesses, kings and wizards
Seeds, shopping baskets and shopping
Space and rockets.

Closely observed, boys appear to be usually busy, but they are busy doing certain things. The interpretation of what they are doing depends upon the context in which it is viewed. I was lucky in that the teacher I was observing was male, which meant that the boys worked in an atmosphere where they were not 'different' from the adult role model and had a wider range of roles to choose from. It was possible in the classroom to be both a Power Ranger and Tinkerbell. The male teacher supported free play that ranged across gender stereotypes and the boys could relate to him as a role model. Many of the boys who are taught exclusively by women tend not to relate directly to the experiences they are being offered, usually because the narratives they are expected to enjoy lie within a more female domain. When stories not aimed at them are presented by a female teacher, boys feel unenthusiastic about them. Narratives often contain images of girls or are constructed with reference to the preoccupations of girls. Stories such as *Cinderella, Sleeping Beauty* or *The Swan Princess* strongly present female experience. While there are many books that do feature boys' experience and preoccupations, boys' later reading choices tend to be more constrained than girls'. Boys tend to read non-fiction books with more enthusiasm once they do start to read but many do not enjoy reading at all. A number of studies (among others, Barrs, 1993; Wray, 1997; Millard, 1997; QCA, 1998) have discussed the problem of why boys appear to read less than girls and various explanations have been suggested. These include:

> Lack of positive male role models in the classroom and often at home
> Lack of support for boys' interests such as football and non-fiction
> An emphasis on story rather than non-fiction to create learning opportunities.

The following observations have been noted:

> That boys respond well to structure within the classroom
> That in some instances boys' experiences are not supported in the classroom
> That boys may come to literacy through different routes than girls
> That boys are not praised for what they are already doing well.
> (See QCA 1998)

The phenomenon of the 'aliterate boy', described by Elaine Millard in her book, *Differently Literate* (1997) could be created by a concept of literacy which fails to use boys' strengths appropriately. Millard describes boys who see no value in reading or literacy activities. We need to accept that some boys come to literacy from a different position to girls. Literacy activities rest on a variety of other activities, such as modelling or construction. It could be that boys will become literate through such activities.

If we accept the importance of symbolising activities such as drawing, modelling and construction to acquiring literacy skills, we can see the value of model making for boys. They could be using the modelling activities described in this book in order to develop their narratives and these narratives could provide a foundation for early literacy activity.

Boys are concerned with different narratives to girls. With the boys I observed, these involved complex stories of transformation, including Power Rangers and Batman. This concurs with the findings of Myra Barrs (1988) reported in her article, *Drawing a Story* (p.68):

> Boys' pictures also frequently reflect a preoccupation with television narratives and especially with superhero stories such as 'He-Man' and Transformers.

Barrs also notes that 'boys rather than girls are inclined to go on using picturing rather than storytelling'.

In the observations I made, props were employed to facilitate transformation. For example, boys used capes to provide power and magic to turn themselves into Superhero figures. Boys were preoccupied with the issues of 'baddies and goodies', and were keen not to be baddies. However, as we saw with Captain Hook's hook, sometimes it was the objects that suggested certain roles, as when the shape of the inside of a toilet roll gave the boys the idea of making the hook.

This emphasis on the visual, and on modelling, as a way of describing the world, was borne out by what I saw. For example, I watched Ziyaad make a 'soldier ship'. The model was developed with the flow of his ideas. The ship changed into a 'fighting ship'as the action progressed. By the end, the soldiers in it had changed the ship into a tank. The story was told through the model, not the other way round.

Model making can be a response to a thought already present in children's minds, or the thought can be created as the model is made. Many boys' narratives developed pictorially, in response to what they saw on the page or at the modelling table. This way of seeing the world, of expressing meaning firstly in the visual/spatial medium, is significant. Model making may be a way into communication for some boys. If we apply Vygotsky's model of 'inner speech' we might conclude that in the initial stages of formulating an idea, some boys use non-linguistic forms such as models to describe what they are trying to say. The domain of space provides a better reflection of their inner thoughts than that of language. When literacy is something a child feels to be in accessible, the domain of the third dimension, such as the curve of a piece of cut-out cardboard, provides a space in which to make meaning.

While the girls tended to develop stories and then express their ideas in models, such as Abigail's rainbow fish and princesses, the boys would model in order to discover the story. Many boys were interested in naratives featuring their favourite cartoon characters, or stories involving fighting or transforming. Not that they regarded killing or fighting as real – they simply used them to express action. Boys' stories tend to focus on action, cars, trucks and trains, and on images of transformation. Some narratives included images of Barbie dolls and princesses, while others were preoccupied with soldiers and fighting.

Map making and play

In many of the observations, children would draw the action they wanted to engage in. This might take place in the playground or in a figurative landscape – a place of inner contours and ideas. Children may seek to express their awareness of space on the page. They do this before they become aware that the medium of pen and paper is a containing one. By the age of seven or eight, children are using paper instrumentally, to write and draw within a prescribed structure. Many pre-school children, however, use paper and crayon to express broad concepts. One observation, for example, found Barney drawing the action in the playground. He had drawn a line showing his route around the playground, with some of the play equipment shown on it. Many of the children's drawings covered the entire surface of the paper. Jack's drawing of 'space', for instance, left no part of the paper blank.

We can see the children mapping their actions on the page. Boys especially seem to enjoy drawing their actions in this way. Map making can often be woven in with narrative play; it can also be seen to be a description of active play, as described by in Barrs (1988, p.115), where Ben used maps to represent action and discovered that drawing could represent action.

I observed the power of the 'treasure map' genre with certain children, and noted that it was often used as a way of expressing narrative action, particularly by boys. Map making in the abstract would be a way of expressing play. Although such activity is not traditionally associated with literacy, I would suggest that boys, in particular, might well respond to map making as a way of expressing ideas. Nursery and reception classrooms are generally focused around telling the story and if pictures are encouraged, it is as a way of supporting alphabetic writing. This can be off-putting to the boys who wish to tell the story through drawing or diagrams.

Overleaf is a 'treasure map' made by a five year old boy at home. The map has a clearly defined spatial narrative. The pen has traversed the page and then buckled over as the journey around the page circles and crosses itself. On it are points of rest. Little round circles are clearly one focus point – possibly this is the 'treasure'. And there are other internal points showing the journey from one round circle to another. The journey is punctuated by stops and starts, as if it were part of a railway track. The boy has drawn action, but it is action structured within narrative. He called it 'a treasure map' and folded it to indicate that it was finished (see Figure 7.1).

Over time Wilfie made other maps, which suggests that he was working within a particular genre. All were produced at home, although he had been introduced to the concept of maps at school. He clearly found it a useful 'way in' to describing his ideas and thoughts. Each map is slightly different, but each is a response to the concept of 'treasure map'. It would be fruitful to explore what he meant by each turn of the pen, and what differentiated one map from another.

It would seem that these maps were a 'language' he used to communicate meaning, but this language is not accessible to everyone. The particular 'language of the boy', be it construction or treasure maps, is sometimes mis-read by teachers, unlike readily available discourses, such as drawing a picture of a house or person, or writing their name, to indicate their attempt at literacy or communication. The map might not be 'read' by the teacher for what it is – a form of communication. That the work of boys should be recognised and understood within whatever forms they choose to use, including describing the world through railway tracks or construction, is an urgent issue with regard to their education.

Often their apparently aimless squiggles on the page, or their large box construction, can be baffling to parents and teachers. Models constructed of lego or duplo may be dismantled without ever being interpreted or 'read' correctly by an adult. The activities boys do, including construction activities, need to be valued as activities of equal value to girls' narratives.

Many of the design and construction activities boys engage in appear as important skills in adult life. Architects, IT technicians, advertisers, media related jobs, building jobs and many others call for the skills of construction, play, design and modelling that boys display in the nursery classroom. What is strange is that we currently do not credit and value these skills. They might appear in the 'design and technology' curriculum but they are not valued as skills of *communication*, which could lead to a developed shaping of meaning at age seven. The skills tested at this age are too narrow and rigidly defined to allow many boys to succeed. And there the cycle of under-achievement begins.

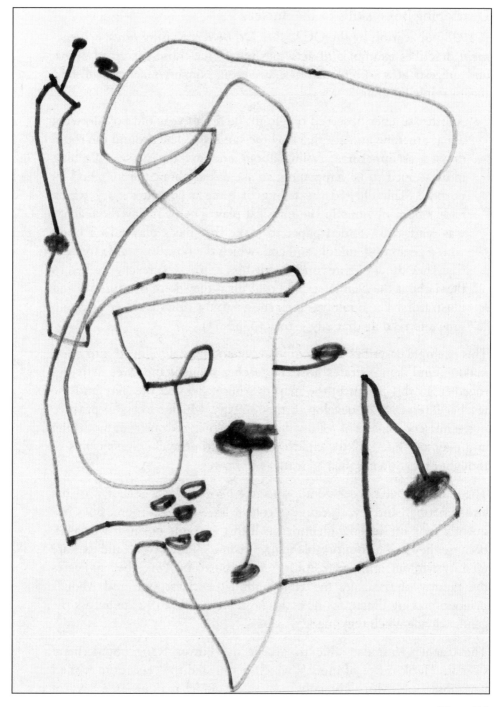

Figure 7.1

Developing boys' skills in the nursery

A 1998 publication by the QCA, *Can Do Better: Raising boys' achievement* describes examples of activities much like those described above and suggests how to refocus boys' attention. Nursery teachers will find this example familiar:

> Another teacher observed one four and a half year old boy drawing a map, then he and another boy the same age flew around the room dressed as Superman, falling about and making noises. Nothing more seemed to be happening, so she asked about the map and its purpose. This elicited the telling of quite a complex story which hadn't been obvious in the physical play. The next day the teacher was ready with folded paper to make that day's play into a book with a beginning, middle and end, which the boys were able to identify. They drew pictures and decided on a title. The teacher talked to them about the characters and told them they were the authors and illustrators. The book was then shown to the other children at group time and read as that day's story (p. 50-51).

This example describes how map making and play developed into book making, and demonstrates how the teacher brought the three activities together. In this instance, the map making generated the play and the teacher intervened to develop further activity. Much successful practice in the nursery consists of following and developing ideas from modelling and play generated by the children, building on the children's trains of thought and allowing their narratives to flower.

The male teacher I observed allowed free play on the theme of warriors and Superman and a wide range of roles within the classroom. Boys frequently took on 'female' identities as if this were the norm. It was as if, because they had a comfortable male role model, the boys could explore identity without inhibition. Andre's decision to be Tinkerbell indicates the fluidity of the roles available within the classroom, and Abdul's princess-making illustrates how the boys were able to range across the gender divide when they made objects.

The teacher was also able to accept the Power Ranger/Spiderman/Captain Hook range of models which permeated the classroom while I was observing. More crucially, he valued model making as a way of communicating something. Boys are often less confident with pen and paper than girls and come to alphabetic literacy later. Model making is a way of expressing ideas in space and extending their thoughts. Joe's Spiderman Ugly Duckling and Robot exemplify ways of expressing concepts in the third dimension. Covering themselves with masking tape

Figure 7.2

took some boys into a wider dimension of using their bodies as a site for expression. Another drawing by Joe, 'The Power Ranger is fighting the baddies', described here, uses strong lines to suggest an active event (see Figure 7.2).

Joe used colour to contrast the Power Ranger with the baddy, and the drawing turns on the clash between the two where he has drawn a squiggly line. Action has been translated onto paper. This drawing became the basis for a narrative and could be developed into project work on Power Rangers. In the classroom I observed, such narratives were encouraged. There was an element of safety in the classroom. Mask making, sword making and armour making all reflected this concern to be safe. Acts of play and story were incorporated into these activities. Boys' interest in growing up in a male environment was encouraged. If teachers build on stories initiated in boys' play, it will result in fuller development by the children of narrative and story. Valuing Power Ranger pictures, and putting them on the walls acknowledged the boys' expressions and desires.

In the QCA book (1998), this observation is born out:

> Boys seem to be influenced by television more than girls, with play often based on television characters and series. Their understanding of the characters appeared to be limited to one characteristic e.g. Superman flies, Turtles fight (QCA *op cit.* p.50).

Many nursery teachers view television play as negative play, as reported in the QCA study (p.13). But valuing boys' interest in cartoon characters and the action based play they develop from it could allow the narratives to develop in a way that could initiate more specific meaning making. Elaine Millard (1997, p.173) argues this point and suggests that older boys could be encouraged to understand the origins of television narrative and to develop work using popular television characters. Mary Hilton (1996, p.44) argues for classrooms that acknowledge specific cultural interests, including the awareness of the gendered nature of so many consumer products.

Boys' model making can be a useful way in to narrative, as the examples of Ziyaad's truck and Joe's Spiderman Ugly Duckling show. This way of working could be continued into the infant curriculum. The example here from the QCA describes how one boy could write only when he had expressed his thoughts through making a model:

> One teacher observed Michael, a six-and-a-half-year-old who has difficulty in beginning to learn to read and write. He is one of the youngest children in his Year 2 group. Last year his Year 1 teacher was sufficiently worried about him to initiate SEN monitoring. His main problem seemed to be a reluctance to engage with print and he frequently became distressed when asked to read or write. His parents were anxious to support him, but were uncertain how to do so.

> In the morning his teacher had asked him to draw and label that day's weather. Michael worked in a group of six children with support. In spite of being in this small group and talking about what the teacher had asked him to do, he found it impossible to comply, becoming increasingly anxious and upset.

> Later in the day he drew a ship, and asked if he could move to the technology area, and make a model. When his model was finished he painted a picture of it, of which he was very proud. When he showed it to his teacher she asked if he would write a story about his ship. He found a piece of pink paper and sat down beside a friendly visitor whom he knew. He wrote very quickly, and in a concentrated, almost

fierce way, sounding out letters and sometimes checking with the adult.

'The bot anD the myc'
The myc waz siln The BOT uv The woT on a sunc oj a The myc puT The ac (up)'

The boat and the monkey
The monkey was sailing the boat over the water on a sunny day and the monkey put the anchor up.

Twice during the writing of this story the teacher announced that it was time to go out to play. Michael continued to write. He could read back his story without hesitation. It has a title, and the episodes are arranged in strict order of time. He was able to discuss his story and talk about what might have happened next. He had been given room to motivate himself and experience success. The contrast with his efforts earlier in the day is marked: the difference between the two writing experiences is striking (QCA, 1998 p.46).

Here a boy has discovered narrative through the process of making a model. He has transposed his ideas from one medium to another. This concept of ideas slipping across modes has been described by Kress (1997) as transduction. If we use the concept of transformation, or transduction across modes, to explain how models such as the Spiderman Ugly Duckling are made and produced, then more credit will be accorded to the activities of boys, and games such as playing Power Rangers need not be seen to be problematic. By building on the skills boys are already exhibiting, a move into literacy through these domains can be achieved. In later years, this can be picked up by using graphic novels. These are stories told through pictures or cartoons, and they are very popular with boys, suggesting that boys may respond more strongly to a visual/spatial element. Boys express concepts through cartoons, models, and three dimensional designs. Narrative and telling stories may be expressed obliquely, through the shape of a cardboard box or the glint of an eye behind a mask. Making swords and gladiators' helmets are activities embedded within a long and complex tradition of story. They are also essential objects of design, and involve an awareness of concepts of shape and solidity.

Implications for practice in nursery schools

- **Valuing boys' culture**
  It is easy to dismiss the action-packed fantasies of boys which derive from cartoons, but it is far batter to interpret them as narratives which can then surface in another medium. When they are made to feel that their interests are valued, boys' construction of meaning becomes possible. Allowing He-Man into the classroom encourages boys to create and develop their narratives.

- **Structuring boys' play**
  Activities can move from play to maps to narrative. Boys' play can often be structured using maps or drawing to develop the action. This can then be described in words and used as the basis for a story. Alternatively, boys' drawings can be seen as an exploration of external spaces, and developed from there into fantasy play.

- **Validate construction activities**
  Most nurseries provide a variety of object-based activities that will develop design and technology skills. Photographs of the models the boys are making can provide a record of their construction activities. If these are interpreted in terms of the narrative and design of the object, the thinking behind the process of making can be validated. Yet many constructions are simply dismantled at the end of a day's session.

- **Follow boys' interests**
  Don't push boys in areas in which they have no interest. Much topic-based work in the nursery is decided upon by external sources. When the topic did not interest the boys I observed, they would resort to 'fighting' to avoid it. Much of the boys' disruptive behaviour I saw was clearly a response to something – generally a lack of activities to hold their attention.

- **Support spatial understandings**
  Present new material spatially, not in narrative form. If material is presented as a model, or in terms of sand, water or construction play, boys will often regard it as useful and interesting. We tend to think always in linguistic and narrative terms when introducing a new topic, yet our experience of the world tells us that new things can also be experienced through objects and through using other senses such as touch or smell. Such an approach can circumvent the common focus on narrative in the early years.

We are only at the beginning of this sort of explorative work. It is important to emphasise that not all boys dislike reading and that many enjoy female narratives such as Barbies and princesses. What I am arguing for is, firstly, recognition that boys may produce different material to girls in the nursery and that this needs to be attended to. Secondly, this material may be presented in a visual/spatial form and that, again, should be acknowledged and built upon. The ideas will often drift across modes to appear in another form. Tracking the flow of boys' activities can produce surprising evidence about their development. Thirdly, the role models available to boys need to be male as well as female. Boys work differently in the company of adult men. The challenge is to change the culture of our schools so that boys' versions of literacy are made possible.

Chapter 8

Home and school
Ideas for teachers and parents

One morning, Martha came in to the nursery proudly bearing a crown and a wand. She announced that they were 'just for showing, before they go home'. Martha then began her morning's modelling. She produced two identical models of a slim, sliver wand. 'This is for home and this is for school', she said. Martha needed to keep the important object, the magic wand, alive in her two separate places where she played. By making two models, she was showing how important she felt the wand to be. Many children found it difficult to let their models go: they would take them home, or miss them if they left them at school. The transition from home to school and back again pre-occupied many of them. Martha had solved the problem by providing herself with identical objects for both places so that she could feel powerful both at home and at school.

My research did not allow me to observe children, other than my own, making models at home. Many children modelled at home, and some-times brought in the results 'to show'. Drawings produced at home might have a slightly different context and produce a different set of meanings in the mind of the child. Barney drew his 'b's' and 'babies' in his bedroom, before bedtime and away from adults (See Figure 5.1), and this may have given the drawings their characteristic of being like 'inner speech'. He was freer to 'talk to himself' while playing at home. Home may be both more chaotic and, possibly, more enabling for children who need to feel secure before they can create.

Many of the activities children do at home are also forms of sign making. A wide variety of phenomena can be studied, such as biscuit making, den making, building toys, play and dressing up. Activities are rooted in everyday life and occur in a more relaxed and less formal way. For example, one child made some biscuits and then a basket to put them in. Here, the idea of 'baskets' was united with the concept of 'biscuits'. A new three dimensional (and edible) sign was being created: 'biscuit in a basket'.

When children are at home they, like adults, like to engage in 'home-making' activities, such as making a den. Dens, while being very messy, are expressions by children of the concept of 'home' and 'intimacy'. Children also like to make houses out of lego, or play 'pretend families' with dolls' houses or in pretend houses in the garden. Although they are not models or drawings, these larger constructions are nonetheless ways of expressing ideas, sometimes for a child on his own, sometimes with friends or carers.

At home children create within a strongly rooted cultural context. They may well be able to express ideas about the worlds away from the nursery, worlds which are unfamiliar to the nursery workers. Children for whom English is not their first language may use their native language to describe their work, and ways of indicating meaning may be freer and more varied than they could be in English.

Family experience can be expressed more freely at home. For example, a family with a new baby might encourage this pre-occupation in the play of the other children, allowing dolls and prams to be used and enjoyed. Some children in the nursery demonstrated their home pre-occupations – others did not. Perhaps we need to pay attention to what children were leaving out of their work, as well as what they put in from home.

Teachers and parents – working together

A challenge for teachers and parents is to unite the two spheres of children's experience: home and school. The cosy, possibly messy and chaotic world of home, with its very different structures and its different influences, could be attended to more, and connected to the often pre-set world of the school nursery. Disney cartoons, for example, could be incorporated into project work. The children's favourite cartoon characters could become regular features of storytelling or modelling sessions. The choice of materials for modelling could include, for instance, the cartoon characters featured on breakfast cereal packets, which children could be encouraged to cut out and develop stories around. Children could discuss the links between selling of cereals and particular toys. Multi-media work using computers and storyboard could be developed using the children's favourite characters. Toys and merchandising based on a favourite show, such as the Teletubbies, could also be incorporated into children's model making. Again, children could reflect on how the selling of such toys links with their own interests and desires, and discuss why they like these characters so much.

Parents are key interpreters for teachers of their children's world. After discussing with parents what activities children enjoy doing at home, the nursery can replicate and respond to the home environment with similar activities at school. A class visit to a local mosque or place of cultural meaning can develop into a discussion about other people's lives and values. New cultural meanings can be explored as a joint project and so become shared. Parents can become involved in such activities. The emphasis must be on developing each child's internal and external worlds so that they begin to cohere. The sense of disconnection between home and school that many children experience need not exist. The challenge is to listen to children and their families and make changes accordingly.

This returns us to the *Desirable Outcomes,* specifically: 'Children talk about where they live, their environment, their families and past and present events in their own lives' (SCAA, 1996). I would suggest that here the emphasis could be extended to: '*Children draw, model or otherwise describe* where they live'. Part of the new understanding gained through this research was that children might not *talk* about their home environment, particularly if English is not their first language, but might, like Mutahhara, *draw* aspects of it. Being sensitive to the drawings and modelling of otherwise silent children is a valuable 'way in' for nursery teachers. The findings described in this book can provide information and approaches that will enhance mutual communication between adults and children.

Parents and support from home – improving practice

Parents can also contribute in new ways to children's creative work by valuing the communication work that their children do. Parents need to take account of what research reveals about the following:

- **The importance of an empty space**
  Adults often want to structure children's work and determine an outcome even before the children begin, when it would be better simply to provide a space to model. This gives children the chance to decide the form and content of their work. The teacher in the nursery provided cardboard boxes of different shapes, glue, scissors, string, masking tape and a table to sit at. No guidance was provided about what would be made or when – that was up to the children. This was hugely facilitative to the model making that I observed.

- **Mess and how to deal with it**

  The playing, cutting out and drawing that children do at home might be regarded by families as just 'mess'. Adults need to distinguish between purposeful mess and the mess that is genuine chaos. It is often unclear what children are doing and why, and their creations get in the way. Many homes aspire to be tidy, ordered places, and parents depend on their own space to recover from the stresses of work. Having their front room turned into a 'den' is unlikely to be popular with tired parents who want to tidy up. But den making is a form of representation, however annoying. Parents have the unenviable task of deciding to share their space with children and let their play invade the space. Both parents and teachers need to distinguish between different sorts of mess. A constant emphasis on 'tidying up' can inhibit children's model making. But parents and teachers need their space and structure too, and a balance needs to be achieved – not total anarchy!

- **The safe space is important**

  Children who do not feel safe often do not dare to draw and model. My observations showed how children created images and objects in situations where they felt safe. They were able to develop what they were doing, and to ask me to help them move the model on. I noticed that children who were new to the nursery or who felt less comfortable in the nursery environment, initially produced less work. Both parents and teachers need to recognise the need to enhance children's sense of safety to support their learning.

- **The importance of listening to children**

  Parents can watch what is being produced, and learn from it. All forms of texts are forms of communication. Parents and teachers are sometimes confronted by a dance, a drawing or a model they cannot understand. Yet most children's work is created within a context – a story, a piece of earlier play, or an experience. Once we hear what children have to say, their model making becomes understandable. Our children tell us things when they draw a squiggle but we are not always aware of what is being said. We need perhaps to pay more attention to our children when they draw, and to listen more closely to what they say about their drawings.

- **Play and modelling**

  The children produced many of the models while working in the same ways as they did when they played. Sometimes they would work together with another child, in an atmosphere of internal concentration. The space between the children and the outside world would be filled with the model. As the children worked, the model held the experience of play. As Ziyaad worked on his 'soldier ship', the play developed. Recognising the value of play and the interwoven nature of the narratives and objects produced around play, the props and the stage sets, will be supportive to children's development. The woven threads of meaning that accompany play and model making can help to develop new thoughts.

Conclusion

The key to understanding children's communication is to recognise how they bring together their internal and external worlds. In order to do their experimental, internal sign making, children need a safe environment in which objects can change in significance. In the familiar world of the home, the curve of a letter can mean a shape that is comprehensible even though it is unfamiliar in school. A piece of Arabic script can carry meaning in the home, yet not at school. Children need to be able to bridge the gap between form and content, filling it with their own meanings. These meanings in turn need to be understood by both teacher and parents. As many studies have shown (eg. Heath, 1983; Taylor, 1983), the connection between home and school must be established if effective literacy learning is to take place.

There is a danger that the world of 'formal education' will take over the nursery. With increasing pressure on schools to open reception classes to four year olds, the possibility arises that children will be expected to trace letters rather than make bracelets, to stop making unstructured sticky models and to start following routine exercises. It must be remembered that to children the model is not unstructured. The model is a product of one child's thought. Increasingly, we evaluate the product and the creator as we would an object we buy in the shops – is it pleasing to us, does it make sense? But children's texts cannot be received in that spirit. They are responses to the world by people who may be looking at different things to adults. When children all produce an identical Easter bunny or Father Christmas or Mother's Day card, the assumption is that the parents will be pleased. The effect is like that of purchasing a new toy. However, for the child, the experience will have been of copying and watching. It may be a valuable experience, but does not compare with experiencing construction for itself.

I am not arguing for something 'woolly' or 'vague'. A classroom can be tightly organised, with teachers who are watchful and who work in a structured way while placing a great deal of the decision making in the hands of the children. Meanings can be made clear in an atmosphere of listening and support. And, although play might create some mess at home, it also creates more communication. Perhaps the current enthusiasm for reading to five year olds for twenty minutes a night should be extended to encouraging twenty minutes of making a den or biscuits or mud pies. We need to understand that these activities will encourage the development of people who one day operate computers, cook meals and design houses.

What children produce needs to be valued by parents, educators and teachers. An untidy home is the bane of some parents' lives, as children make dens, draw or scribble on scraps of paper or cover the living room floor with bits of cut out magazines, but if we can see this as the way that children come to their making activities, it becomes easier to tolerate the mess. We need to be able to distinguish between productive mess and mess that is simply chaos – this book indicates where the productive mess lies. Teachers, particulary if they are in the throes of an OFSTED inspection, might, similarly, not want to let their pupils make Spiderman models covered in masking tape or play wildly, because the links between different activities may not be obvious. Perhaps we need to remind the inspectors where literacy comes from and how meaning can be generated in a variety of modes.

The experience of parenting and the observation of children in the nursery has shown how one can unpack children's activities. Closely observing the work children do, be it scribbling or making play houses, provides insights into the flow of children's thoughts. It is this informed and close observation that makes the process rigorous. As the complexity of simple acts, such as the creation of a rainbow fish, is unravelled, we can see from the resulting object the mental processes involved. And these mental processes are as complex as the skills which enable a child to write a story or read a book. Engaging in these mental processes builds up enormously important skills for the future. The challenge for adults is to recognise and harness the work by which children develop those skills. By watching and analysing children's work, we can obtain the key to helping children with this vital task.

Select Bibliography

Armstrong, M. (1980) *Closely Observed Children*. London: Writers and Readers Press

Barrs, M. 'Maps of Play' in Meek, M. and Mills, C. (Eds) (1988) *Language and Literacy in the Primary School*. Lewes: Falmer Press

Barrs, M. 'Drawing a Story' in Lightfoot, M. and Martin, N. (Eds) (1988) *The Word for Teaching is Learning*. Oxford: Heinemann Educational Books

Barrs, M. and Pidgeon, S. (1993) *Reading the Difference*. London: CLPE

Barton, D. (1994) *Literacy: an introduction to the ecology of written language*. Oxford UK and Cambridge USA: Blackwell

Bissex, G. L. (1980) *Gyns at Wrk: a child learns to write and read*. Cambridge, Mass: Harvard University Press

Bussis, A. M and Chittenden, E. *et al.* (1985) *Inquiry Into Meaning: an investigation of learning to read*. Hillsdale, N.J.: Lawrence Erlbaum Associates

Carle, E. (1987) *The Tiny Seed*. London: Hodder and Stoughton

Campbell, R. (1996) *Literacy in Early Education*. Stoke on Trent: Trentham Books

Dyson, A.H. (1993) *Social Worlds of Children Learning to Write*. New York: Teachers College Press

Ferreiro, E. and Teberosky, A (1982) *Literacy before Schooling*. London: Heinemann Educational Books

Geertz, C. (1973) *The Interpretation of Cultures*. New York: Basic Books Inc.

Geertz, C. (1983) *Local Knowledge*. New York: Basic Books Inc.

Hall, N. and Robinson, A. (1995) *Exploring Writing and Play in the Early Years*. London: Fulton

Hall, N. and Martello, J. (1996) *Listening to Children Think: exploring talk in the early years*. London: Hodder and Stoughton

Halliday, M.A.K. (1979) *Language as Social Semiotic: the social interpretation of language and meaning*. London: Edward Arnold

Heath, S. B. (1983) *Ways with Words: Language, life and work in communities and classrooms.* Cambridge: Cambridge University Press

Hilton, M. (1996) *Potent Fictions: children's literacy and the challenge of popular culture.* London: Routledge

Kress, G. and van Leeuwen, T. (1996) *Reading Images: the grammar of visual design.* London: Routledge

Kress, G. (1997) *Before Writing: rethinking the paths to literacy.* London: Routledge

Nutbrown, C. (1994) *Threads of Thinking: young children learning and the role of early education.* London: Paul Chapman

Millard, E. (1997) *Differently Literate: boys, girls and the schooling of literacy.* London: Routledge

Paley, V. G. (1980) *Wally's stories.* Cambridge, MA: Harvard University Press

Paley, V. G. (1986) *Mollie is three: growing up in school.* Chicago, University of Chicago Press

Qualifications and Curriculum Authority (1998) *Can do better: Raising boys' achievements in English.* London: QCA

School Curriculum and Assessment Authority (1996) *Desirable Outcomes for Children's Education on Entering Compulsory Education.* DfEE/SCAA

Taylor, D. (1983) *Family Literacy: young children learning to read and write.* Exeter: Heinemann

Vygotsky, L.S. (1978) *Mind in Society: the development of higher psychological processes.* Cambridge, Mass: Harvard University Press

Vygotsky, L.S. (1986) *Thought and Language.* Massachusetts: Massachusetts Institute of Technology (notably the chapter: 'Thought and Word')

Whitehead, M. R. (1990) *Language and Literacy in the Early Years.* London: Paul Chapman

Winnicott, D. W. (1971) *Playing and Reality.* Middlesex: Penguin (notably the chapter: 'Transitional objects and transitional phenomena')

Index

affect 7-8
alphabet 2, 6
    animation of 69-70
    in children's names 56-8, 60, 65-70
    kinaesthetic appreciation of 51
    shape 85
animation 69
    and cutting out 39-41, 45
    and letters 58, 69-70
Armstrong, M. 16

Barrs, M. 58-9, 89, 90, 91
Barbie dolls 83, 99
Barton, D. 49
Batman 24, 51, 83, 88, 90
Bissex, G.L. 3
boys 2, 3, 48
    and meaning making 87-99
Bussis, A. M. 16

Captain Hook 10, 26, 88, 90, 94
Carle, E. 18
chador 48, 74, 75, 76, 79, 82, 84
Chittenden, E. 16
Cinderella 27, 75-76, 82-3, 84, 85, 88
communication 2, 6, 8, 105
composing 4, 6, 8, 82-4
concept formation 31
Cruella de Vil 13, 45, 48, 83
culture 8, 73-4, 82-5
    home 75, 82-5, 86, 102
    school 49, 76-83
cutting out 37-41, 45, 53

design 7, 8, 15, 31, 51, 92, 98
Disney 75, 76, 79, 83, 84, 102
drawing 15, 17, 41-2, 46-7, 91-2, 94-5, 98
    home environment 103
    and literacy 3-4, 28, 56-7, 58-9, 63, 71, 83, 84, 89
Dyson, A.H. 4, 58, 83, 84

externalisation 30, 84

fairytale 24, 75, 84
Ferreiro, E. 3
Fox, C. 4

Geertz, C. 13, 14, 73, 85
group processes 28-9, 85

Hall, N. 5
Halliday, M.A.K. 36
Heath, S.B. 49, 105
Hilton, M. 5, 96
home 2, 3, 7, 101-5
    and school 31, 32, 40-1
    mess 101, 104
inner speech 30-1, 101
internal concepts 1, 5, 18-21, 30, 69, 80-1
internalisation 17, 30, 81, 84
intertextuality 5, 83
Islamic heritage 79

Kress, G 6, 23, 27, 39, 45, 52, 58, 69, 81-2, 97

literacy 3-6, 7, 14, 18, 35-6, 49-51, 55, 60, 70, 84, 89, 99, 106

The Little Mermaid 83

map makding 47, 91-2, 94, 98
Martello, J. 5
Mary Poppins 83
mask making 28, 43, 47-8,
    and boys 95, 97
media 24, 82-4
Millard, E. 89, 96
modelling 1, 2, 6-8, 17-24, 35-37, 41, 44, 45, 48-9, 50-3, 82, 97-8, 102, 103
    and boys 89-90, 92, 96-7
modes 5, 6-7, 13, 17, 32, 97, 99, 106
multi-media 4, 12, 102
    multi-modal
    meaning making 5-6
    texts 12, 32, 97

narratives 4, 27, 50-1, 82, 89-91, 95-8
National Literacy Strategy 55
nursery 2, 6, 11, 14-15, 74, 88, 94
Nutbrown, C. 14-15

observation 2, 9-10, 13-16, 106

Paley, V.G. 4
parents 1, 8, 9, 14-16, 27, 85, 104
Peter Pan 10, 26, 27, 51, 82
Piagetian thought 3
play 1, 3, 4, 5, 6, 8, 10, 13, 17, 27-8, 42,
    47-9, 83, 91
    and boys 94-5
    and modelling 104-5
    and writing 58, 70
playgroups 9
Power Rangers 24, 85, 88, 94-5, 97
Princess Diana 75, 76, 84
princesses 13, 28, 40, 75-9, 82, 84, 88,
    94, 99
psychoanalysis 8

The Rainbow Fish 27, 51
reading 49, 61, 62, 69
    as transforming action 74, 81-2
representation 5, 6-8, 15, 31
Robinson, A. 5

QCA (formerly SCAA) 11, 70-1, 89, 94,
    96, 103

schemas 14-15, 43
school 2, 3, 6, 55, 101, 102, 103, 105
semiotics 5, 7
siblings 8, 102
signs 7, 27-8, 36, 84
    making 31, 82, 101-2
Sleeping Beauty 75, 79,
space
    the body and space 41-7
Spice Girls 83
Spiderman 13, 24, 27, 51, 82, 88, 94, 96,
    97, 106
stories 4, 7, 17, 49-50, 71, 82, 97
Superman 52, 83, 94
symbolising 8, 28, 52, 58, 63
Swan Princess 75

talk 4, 17, 27, 32, 48, 49, 104
Taylor, D. 105
teachers 14-15, 27, 32, 50, 105
Teberosky, A. 3
Teletubbies 82, 83, 102
television 17, 24, 50, 96
texts
    analysis of 5, 6, 8
    as communication 15, 104-5
    multimedia 4-5
Tinkerbell 10, 26, 83, 88, 94
The Tiny Seed 18, 20, 27, 30, 50
toys 102-3
transduction 27, 97
transformations 18, 23, 24, 32, 80, 81,
    85, 90, 91, 97
transformed
    into other forms 24-6
    through disguises 40, 45
    signs 27-8
transitional object 31

The Ugly Duckling 24, 51, 85, 88

Vamp 48
van Leeuwen, T. 7
The Very Hungry Caterpiller 85
videos 8, 17, 32, 50, 82, 83
Vygotsky, L.S. 30, 49, 58, 81, 90

Whitehead, M.R. 58, 84
Winnicott, D.S. 31
Wray, D. 89
writing 3, 4, 8, 56-9, 61, 65-9, 70-1